A Short History of
American Religious Folk Song

Somber Psalm Tunes,
Camp-Meeting Hymns,
& Shape-Note Socials

George Pullen Jackson

edited by
Kevin I. Slaughter

HOLLOW SQUARE BOOKS
Baltimore

A Short History of American Religious Folk Song: Somber Psalm Tunes, Camp-Meeting Hymns, and Shape-Note Socials
Designed and edited by Kevin I. Slaughter
"Editor's Statement" © 2025 Kevin I. Slaughter

The body of this work constitued the first half of
White and Negro Spirituals, Their Lifespan and Kinship
(New York: J.J. Augustin, 1943), by George Pullen Jackson.
The appendix "Buckwheat Notes" by George Pullen Jackson
originally appeared in *The Musical Quarterly*,
Vol. 19, No. 4 (Oct., 1933), pp. 393-400.

The editor gives thanks to the *Shenandoah Harmony*
singing clan of Virginia, and everyone who lifts up
their voice around the hollow square.

Hollow Square Books
Baltimore, July 2025
978-1-943687-37-4

Editor's Statement

This volume presents a carefully adapted edition of a seminal work by esteemed musical scholar and historian George Pullen Jackson (1874–1953). Jackson made significant contributions to the study of American religious music, particularly through his research on shape-note singing and the books associated with Sacred Harp traditions. Before his groundbreaking 1933 study, *White Spirituals in the Southern Uplands*, this musical tradition had largely faded from national awareness. His work played a key role in rekindling scholarly and public interest in this uniquely American form of religious song.

The book you now hold is adapted from *White and Negro Spirituals, Their Lifespan and Kinship* (1943), in which Jackson examines the evolution of American religious folk music. The book is, essentially two complete, but complimentary essays, gathered into one binding. However, the original title alone presents challenges for reprinting in today's market, as the term "Negro," though standard in Jackson's time, is now widely recognized as outdated and problematic. Beyond its title, the second half of *White and Negro Spirituals* focuses on Jackson's theories regarding the origins of what were once commonly called "Negro spirituals"—particularly his argument that much of this music was derived from European sources. These theories have not stood the test of time and remain controversial.

This edition includes only the first half of Jackson's work, which remains a rich and insightful account of the development of American religious folk traditions, offering valuable historical context for scholars and enthusiasts alike. In preparing this edition, I have focused on removing references to the second half of Jackson's book while making only minor editorial adjustments elsewhere.

When historically dated terminology—such as "Negroes"—appears in direct quotations, I have chosen to preserve it in its original context. This term was once a neutral descriptor for Black Americans, though it often carried implicit biases. For example, on page 120, a direct quotation from the *Louisville Courier* (1840s) includes an offensive racial slur and other language used to belittle all attendees of a Millerite revival. The same slur is again printed in the appendix. While such language may be jarring to modern readers, its inclusion reflects the prejudices of its time and provides historical context.

During the preparation of this text for publication, I spoke with several people about my plans. The reactions were as extreme as I might have expected. "People should understand he was a man of his time," one said, dismissively. Another told me, "I think it's too problematic." While I'm inclined to agree, at least in part, with the first statement—and I don't believe any writer is "too problematic" to be read or learned from—both reactions risk allowing valuable and enjoyable work to be lost to time: one through defensiveness, the other through fear. Jackson was, of course, a man of *his* time. But readers are of *their own*. This adaptation may serve its intended purpose—or perhaps it will satisfy no one.

By presenting this material in a new form, I aim to make Jackson's valuable historical insights more accessible while acknowledging the ways in which both scholarship and language have evolved.

Kevin I. Slaughter
Baltimore, April 30, 2025

Contents

Editor's Statement 3

Old English Dissent Breaks Out in American Colonies 7
Song Purveyors to "Great Awakening" Mean Well .. 17
A Free Folk Takes Religion in Hand 28
Freedom in Religion Begets Freedom in Singing. ... 42
The Carnal Lover Is Plundered of His Tunes....... 77
Camp Meetings Are Bred in Old Kentucky. 91
"Crazy" Lorenzo Dow 104
Farmer William Miller Dates the World's End 117
Songs of the Second Coming.................. 125
Shakers, Mormons Ride the Millennial Wave 129
Revival Spiritual Tunes Come Into the Open...... 139
Old-Time Religion Outmoded. 147
Old-time Songs Are Pushed Aside 156

Appendix
Buckwheat Notes 167

Sacred harp convention in Cullman, Alabama, July 1, 1943. Youthful Mary Kitchens Gardner (left center) of Jasper, Alabama, leads a "lesson." *The Sacred Harp*—the singers' and their ancestors' musical "bible" for a hundred years—is a unique repository of early American religious folk songs. *Photograph by Joe Overton, Birmingham, Alabama.*

Old English Dissent Breaks Out in American Colonies

The highlight of the revolutionary century in American history was its anti-institutionalism. The colonies were filling up fast with those who despised establishments, those they had fled from and those they met here. And they met a plenty of them, economic, political, social, religious,—all close knit, colony by colony (excepting perhaps in one or two middle colonies); unyielding establishments which bred dissent fast and gave the dissenters in due time a place to live where, as they weened, the least established was the best established.

It was the colonial religious institutions that proved to be among the most unyielding and thus the most prolific breeders of dissent. And this phase of eighteenth century life is so important and so fundamental to our chief concern here—the unique songs of religious dissent—that we must outline it at once.

First let us make clear that we are not discussing religion or dissent from religion. Religion is probably coeval with man. But if it is defined simply as the belief in and the veneration of a supreme being, it can hardly be called an institution any more than we can call the love of man for woman or of man for his neighbor an institution. A particular man-formulated organization for the fostering of the religious urge is, however, quite a different thing. It *is* an institution, and it goes through the life cycle—birth, youth, maturity, decline, death—of man-made establishments as such. It is organizations of this sort which we are to discuss.

The Christian Church is one of the longest-lived religious institutions, that is, if we regard it as a whole along with its Jewish forerunner. If however we consider Judaism, Romanism, Greek Orthodoxism, Anglicanism, early European Protestantism and later American Protestantism as distinct though related, then the life span of each becomes shorter and more easily observable. We shall so regard them.

Christian religious institutions have been particularly vulnerable to the virus of dissent. I think of two reasons for this. One, because the Bible, their one basic authority, is such a baffling document or such an "elaborate oriental literature," as Thomas Cuming Hall characterizes it,[1] that it breeds endlessly varying interpretations. Two, even though once satisfyingly interpreted, such interpretation fails to satisfy in the long run and simply because the Bible and its supposedly definitive interpretation are vitally concerned not only with the *origins* of things and man (which may be looked on as fairly static whatever they really were) but also with the unfolding *history* of man and with his *destiny*, in both of which there is apparently nothing so persistent as change. Hence the ever present demand for change in any and all interpretations of that human destiny. Those who remain true to a Christian institution and its scriptural explanations of human life are believers, conformists, the faithful, the orthodox. Those who vary in thought, word or deed from the instituted norm become heretics, protestants, dissenters, puritans, deluded ones, schismatics and what have you.

Dissent has appeared in different guises among

---

1   *The Religious Background of American Culture*, Boston, 1930, p. 88.

JONATHAN EDWARDS, 1703–1758, Massachusetts preacher whose revivalistic zeal set the Great Awakening fires. From an oil painting by Joseph Badger.

different peoples at different times and has ushered in different institutional changes and indeed different institutions themselves. We are concerned here with a few of those dissent guises because they are fundamental to our first and one of our chief considerations—the religious aspects of early America.

Dissent from the historical Christian Church assumed an important and peculiar guise under the leadership of Martin Luther. Beginning as a German-nationally characterized uprising against papal abuses of power and making its appeal to large segments of the nation, it soon found itself forced into the protective arms and the directive control of temporal princes and thus into a growing historical-institutional formality.

Another important group of dissenters, emerging almost at the same time, was led by John Calvin. This more folky group demurred notably from the Lutherans' attachment to temporal governments. It insisted on "freedom of religion." And it was such freedom from princely protection which, whenever and wherever maintained, seems to have led to their persecution, to their becoming scattered over many lands on the continent and in Britain, and to their splitting up into many sects.

Both of these dissenting groups appear in the early American picture. The Calvinists came hither largely by way of Britain and appear as the Presbyterians who settled chiefly in the middle colonies, and as the Congregationalists of New England where they became the Standing Order. The Lutheran variety of continental Protestantism came direct to the New World with the Germans and other northern European settlers and spread largely over the Pennsylvania and New Jersey region.

A third dissentist movement, much earlier than those mentioned above and more significant than either of them from our point of view, was Old English dissent. It was that native force which has erupted periodically from the time of Wyclif and the Lollards (who ignited also the continental Hussite fires) down to John Wesley and his field preachers and since. Like the continental varieties it was a protest, though perhaps not always recognized as such, of the native or national against that which was foreign. But less like the Lutheran and Calvinist brands, it has usually centered in the lower, greater, incoherent masses. Old English dissent must be defined therefore as a recurrent *folk* movement.

(Both Anglicanism and Roman Catholicism came to America and became important components of the early religious picture. The Catholics were strong in Maryland and the Anglicans became the Established Order in Virginia and elsewhere in the south. All this is well known and is mentioned here chiefly to remind the reader that the American dissenter found his enemies right at home.)

It was a variety of the Old English dissentist turn of mind, of course, which brought over the early New Englanders. But with the passing of the decades the tables were turned; the New England dissenters, in erecting their Standing Order, invited dissent—the same Old English sort—from *their own* ranks. Their power as *ins* gave birth to *outs*—those American dissenters *from* dissenters who became in time articulate and numerous.

The fact that dissent is comparatively neglected by the historians must not lead to a belief that it is unimportant. That would be the opposite of the truth. Hall, for one historical philosopher, looks on the Anglo-American "dissenting mind" as one of the most important elements in the forming of American culture, and he attributes the historians' comparative silence on the subject to the difficulties they meet when they try to peer into the darkness of the undocumented "nine-tenths of life."

On the following pages of this chapter I shall attempt

to review an important outbreak of dissentism in America (with less emphasis on its aspects in Britain) in the eighteenth century. And I shall try to show, in subsequent chapters, the close relationship of rampant dissent both to the Revolutionary struggle and to the post-Revolutionary cultural confusions in the young nation. I shall do this because I look on the early religious eruptions as the real ground out of which American religious folk song grew.

Dissent thrives on institutional oppression. During the four to five decades before the Revolution the dissenting colonist felt dissatisfied with and oppressed by all the brands of instituted religion: by the Congregational Standing Order in New England, by the strait-laced Presbyterian and Lutheran creeds and practices in the middle colonies and by the Established Order in the south. All these groups were, as appears from the records, rather weak spiritually. But they were still institutions and they were linked, in the northeast and the south at least, with the magistracy. This gave them their power to oppress and persecute, a power which they used generously, as numbers of church historians have made abundantly clear.

But the dissenter began in time to feel his own power. People of his turn of mind came from everywhere. From England came the Quakers, Sandemanians, English Moravians, Baptists, and later the Shakers. And even among those who were nominally Presbyterians and Congregationalists or Independents, there developed, as we know, a big element of dissent. From the mainland of Europe came the German Mennonites, Reformed, Moravian Brothers; from France and the lands into which they had been driven, the Huguenots.

Not only the religious dissenters flocked hither. There came also those who dissented from *all* religion,—the Deists or free thinkers. European and British rationalism had bred what might be called radical intellectual dissent. The New World was a favorable soil for such freedom-from-religion thought and the non-religious mind sided naturally, though for different reasons, with the religious dissenting mind against the common enemy, religious institutionalism.

It is important to remember also that the religious dissenters here, as ever in English life, were the poor, the at first politically powerless, the socially "wrong people," and that they remained so for a long time. This was most strikingly evident in the south where the "right people" of the Established Order owned all the good tobacco land and most of the slaves. This general economic-political-social disability kept the dissenters long in the handicrafts and trades and/or drove them to the backwoods and frontiers.

I have called attention to the incoherent nature of dissent, as such, and the disunity of dissenters. This was true of them also in America. There was, however, one factor which tended gradually to unite them, in mind at least—the *Great Awakening*. The religious movement bearing this name was never a unit institutionally. It was rather a number of religious-freedom fires which ignited as it would seem by spontaneous combustion along the row of colonies and raged intermittently throughout a long generation before the Revolutionary War and another generation after. The chroniclers picture these fires as set by individuals—Jonathan Edwards, Theodore Frelinghuysen, George Whitefield, the Tennents, Samuel Davies, Shubael Stearns, and others. I would say rather that these poked and tended them. Edwards heaped fuel on the freedom fires in New England; Frelinghuysen and the Tennents, in New Jersey and eastern Pennsylvania; Whitefield roved all along the seaboard; and Stearns tended the Baptist bonfires in North Carolina.

Practically everything these evangelists did was highly offensive to instituted religion. They romped over all denominational lines, preached wherever they could get a crowd (even where their own denomination and the laws of the land forbade such activity), held extravagantly emotional revivals (shocking to staid intellectual institutionalists), spread Arminianism or salvation for all through faith (scandalizing the predestinarian Congregationalists, "Particular" Baptists and Presbyterians), spread "believers'" baptism (weakening thus the traditional, institutional rite of baby baptism), and did everything possible to dissuade people from "indulging in pride and fashions, vain talking and jesting, cursing and swearing, drunkenness, adultery, carnal company, gaming, frolicking and dancing, anger, malice, revenge, worldly-mindedness, worldly honors, rabbi-greetings(?), uppermost rooms(?) and chief seats—choosing all or any of these is choosing the way to hell."[2]

One of the best stories of early revival scenes was told by Charles Chauncey in his *Seasonable Thought upon the State of Religion in New England*, published in Boston, 1743. He told about the astounding carryings-on by the Great Awakening preachers and congregations during the revivals started in 1735 by Jonathan Edwards.

The Edwardeans, according to Chauncey, believed in "taking the kingdom of heaven by storm." "Be violent for the kingdom" and maybe you'll be saved. James Davenport, a wild preacher from Southold, Massachusetts, wound up his sermons by shouting, "Now, now, now you are going right into the bottom of hell!" After a short prayer he called the "distressed" into the front seats. "Then he came out of the pulpit and stript off his upper garments and got up into the seats and leapt up and down some times and clapt his hands together and cried out these words: 'The war goes on, the fight goes on, the devil goes down, the

---

[2] From a Freewill Baptist *Circular Letter* sent out from a New Gloucester, Maine, quarterly meeting in the 1780s, as cited by I. D. Stewart, *The History of the Freewill Baptists for Half a Century*. Dover, (New Hampshire), 1862, p. 78f.

devil goes down!' and then betook himself to stamping and screaming most dreadfully."

Chauncey told also of another heavenstormer and how, after a little "sufficiently terrible" preaching, there was "some commotion among the young women." This response raised his steam pressure. He poured terrors on them. Half a dozen of them "were presently thrown into hysterical fits." They calmed down when he did. They threw fits again when he whooped 'er up. "Sometimes he put a mighty emphasis on little unmeaning words" with the same effect on his hearers as when an "awful truth" was uttered.

The same chronicler calls attention to an account (appearing in No. 391 of the *Boston Post Boy*) of how every itinerant preacher warned his hearers that they were the only ones still unsaved, "that hellfire flashes in their faces and that the devil now stands ready to carry them down to hell; and that they (the preachers) will often times repeat the awful word, 'Damned! Damned! Damned!'"

James Davenport was charged before the General Assembly of Connecticut, and the charge was sustained, that he terrified the people "(1) by pretending some extraordinary discovery and assurance of the very near approach of the end of the world; (2) by indecent and affected imitation of the Agony and Passion of our Blessed Saviour."

Jonathan Edwards and George Whitefield, though extremely emotional, were real preachers. But very soon "there appeared large numbers of lay exhorters, men of all occupations who were vain enough to think themselves fit to be the teachers of others, people of no learning and small capacities, babes in age as well as understanding, chiefly young persons, sometimes lads or rather boys— nay women and girls—even negroes."[3]

---

3   The quotations are from Sam P. Hays' article on "Edwardean Revivals," *American Journal of Psychology*, xiii, 550-574. See especially p. 560ff.

The reaction of the religious intellectuals is nicely illustrated by "the testimony of the Faculty of Harvard College against George Whitefield, December 28, 1744," as cited by the noted Baptist evangelist Jacob Knapp just a hundred years afterward. "We look upon his going about in this itinerant way, especially as he has so much of an enthusiasticated (quite irrational) turn of mind, (as being) utterly inconsistent with the peace and order, if not the very being of these churches of Christ." The Harvard men are quoted as accusing Whitefield also of being a "censorious and slanderous man" who picked especially on the settled clergy, and of actual dishonesty in the expenditure of money collected for the orphan house in Savannah, Georgia. Yale College, too, joined in the accusations, according to Elder Knapp's citation: "He had spoken uncharitably of the colleges, and other ministers, saying that unconverted ministers were half beast and half devil, and that they could no more be the means of any man's conversion, than a dead man could beget living children."[4]

The widespread and emotional Great Awakening was, as we have said, never coherent. For fifty years it remained quite non-institutional. Its converts did, however, take on (or were given) the general name "New Lights." They were dissenters from all authority, civil, religious, economic, and social. The Tories jailed their roving leaders when they could catch them and penalized the people for merely listening to their preaching.

But all this, the rantings and the persecutions, receded when the struggle for political freedom began. I shall have more to say on that subject presently. But first I wish to review, on the following pages the attempts of the pre-Revolutionary religious dissenters to find or make songs for their new-found religious life and doings.

---

[4] *The Evangelical Harp.* Jacob Knapp. Utica, (New York), 1845, 204f.

Song Purveyors to "Great Awakening" Mean Well But Muddle

> Lord be praised for thy work
> In the Jersey's and New York!
> —Joseph Humphreys, 1743

If the New Lighters had good reason for religious rebellion they had even better reason for general dissent from the singing practices of the Standing Order. All British and American Protestant congregations sang psalms, that is, if they sang at all. The tunes were mostly leftovers from those once imported into the British Isles along with continental Protestantism from the European mainland. They are known to have been based, in the earliest times of their use, on German and French secular folk tunes. But no folk ever sang secular tunes like those heard in the American colonial meeting houses of the early eighteenth century. Whatever spirit, rhythm and melody they may once have had—all these had disappeared.

Why had they fled? Why was singing of those same tunes which had once delighted even the pampered Parisian court précieux now described as "the braying of asses?"

The consensus seems to be that the downfall of the psalms was due largely to a chronic indifference on the part of Protestants in the British Isles and then in America. Preaching and praying were considered essential. Singing was decidedly secondary in importance. Another reason for the psalms' plight, valid especially but not exclusively in the American colonies, was that country (as opposed to urban) conditions prevailed. For the masses that meant little education in letters and none in music. For those many who could not read, the psalms had to be "lined out" (one or two lines at a time) by a deacon and "set" (intoned) by the same functionary. This limping alternation combined with other factors to bring the singing to an unbelievably slow pace. "I have myself," declared Thomas Walter, a young song reformer of the 1720s, "paused twice on one note to take breath." And along with this deathly slow pace came other aberrations. Since it is impossible for the natural human voice to hold a single note-syllable through two breaths, numerous variations or tonal interpolations appeared. And thus the tune, as the one time printed notes may have delineated it, lost character,—lost even the semblance of a tune. And its rhythm, if we may call it rhythm, became the gait of the slowest of the slow singers.

It was this absence of direction, control and cultivation of group singing, this lack of concern with song as such which had, in the run of perhaps two centuries, resulted in a condition which was musically about as far from what the English folk would normally sing individually, *did* normally sing in other environments, as one could imagine.

The Edwardean and Whitefieldian revivals, nevertheless, had to get along, in their early phases at least, with the old psalm tradition in singing manner and song. All records point to this conclusion. But there were signs of a new manner of song even then, that is, in the 1730s and 1740s. The revivalists could sing, if they would, new texts if not new tunes. Young Isaac Watts, a hymnody rebel himself, had only a short while before provided a great stock, not only of hymns founded on psalms but of others based on the New Testament, cast in good old English stanzaic patterns. It was chiefly from this store that the singing masses of America adopted in time large numbers of hymns and made them their own. Then came the Wesleys with an even greater torrent of religious lyrics for dissenters.

But texts, folky or otherwise (and they were usually otherwise), aren't songs. They are as good as unborn as long as they lack proper tunes. It was suitable tunes that the Great Awakening at first lacked. John Wesley saw this plainly. No powerful religious movement, he knew, could do without a suitable body of song. So he went about consciously trying to provide the badly needed tunes. He knew how Luther had provided his great religious movement with a magnificent body of song. He knew probably also that the music of that corpus had been borrowed from the German folk. And this seems to have led him to the false reasoning, so often observed in Anglo-Saxon thought on cultural matters, that if foreign song was good for foreigners it should be good also for the English. We might assume charitably that he knew nothing of the great body of English and Gaelic folk tunes still echoing in the British Isles as they had echoed since the times of the ancient bards. A more realistic view, however, would be that he knew that music but despised it. Be that as it may, he resolved to ignore what was at hand and borrow from afar,—to provide the religious awakening with German tunes. These he found notably among the new-come Moravians who were just then taking root in English soil.

To selections from this stock of German Moravian tunes Wesley added airs by Haendel, Giordani, Giardini, Lampe and other composers of the imported elite London musical circle, and it was this hodgepodge of everything but good old English song that made up his first tune book for the Methodists. *A Collection of Tunes, Set to Music, as They Are Commonly Sung at the Foundery*, London, 1742, and set the pace for that upsurging group in its early

GEORGE WHITEFIELD, 1714–1770, English Calvinistic Methodist preacher who took the torch from Jonathan Edwards and carried the fires of the New Awakening to all the American colonies. His legions of converts, "New Lights," became the prime forces in the free, folky, religious life of the young Republic. The statue by R. Tait McKenzie once stood on the University of Pennsylvania campus.

stages of growth. Thus Wesley consciously, but without realizing the consequences of his act, got the singing of his religious movement in Great Britain off on the wrong foot.

It wouldn't have been so bad if the Wesleys had been of less influence,—if they had not given their long and energetic lives to institutionalizing their folkfootless hymnody. It would have been still worse for Americans, however, if the Wesleyan influence in song had not all but refused to cross the Atlantic, and if that modicum of influence which did reach these shores had not been spurned here by the singing masses of dissenters.[5]

The only piece among the Wesley-borrowed and specially composed songs which enjoyed long currency among American country singers in the mass was *Old German*. Its very aloneness goes to uphold the thesis of the futility of going to other peoples and other lands, even to musical Germany, for songs for the masses to sing.

OLD GERMAN[6]

All glo - ry and praise to the An - cient of Days
Who was born and was slain to re - deem a lost race.

While the Wesleys, despite their good intentions, got

---

5   This is precisely the opposite of the view held by most authorities on early Wesleyan music. I hope the reader will charitably overlook my own earlier sanction of the "authoritative" view that J. Wesley was the legitimate father of the early religious folk-hymn movement. (*Cf. Spiritual Folk Songs of Early America*, p. 6.) That was before I had been able to find out facts for myself. I am now convinced that the religious folk songs did not have a Methodist parentage.

6   John Wesley borrowed the tune and translated the text from English Moravians' German book. As to its long use in America see *Spiritual Folk-Songs*, No. 104, and *Down-East Spirituals*, No. 134.

their song movement off to a bad start, another worker (in the Evangelical wing of dissent) did better. Young John Cennick (1718–1755) was destined to become the real founder of folky religious song in the rebellious eighteenth century movement. This Quaker-become-Methodist (and later, even Moravian) preacher was scarcely of age when his *Sacred Hymns for the Children of God* appeared;[7] and two years later he brought out his *Sacred Hymns for the Use of Religious Societies, Generally Composed in Dialogues*.[8] This latter booklet seems to mark the actual start, in England, of homespun hymns in the Great Awakening.

Its chief contribution was Cennick's "Jesus My All to Heaven is Gone" which was to become one of the most widely sung religious lyrics among the country folk of America during the entire 200 years which have now passed since it appeared.[9]

> Jesus, my all, to heaven is gone,
> He that I placed my hopes upon.
> His tracks I see and I'll pursue
> The narrow way till him I view.
> The way the holy prophets went,
> The road that leads from banishment,
> I'll go, for all his paths are peace,
> The King's highway of holiness.
> *No stranger may proceed therein,
> No lover of the world and sin,
> No lion, no devouring care,
> No ravenous tyger shall be there.
> *No, nothing may go up thereon
> But travelling souls, and I am one.
> Wayfaring men to Canaan bound

---

7 Date of first edition unknown. Second edition, London, 1741.

8 Bristol, 1743.

9 For references to its astoundingly wide use in country song in America see my *White Spirituals*, p. 222f.

> Shall only in the way be found.
> *Nor fools by carnal men esteem'd
> Shall err therein, but they redeem'd
> In Jesus' blood, shall shew their right
> To travel there till heaven's in sight.
> This is the way I long have sought,
> And mourned because I found it not;
> My grief my burden long has been,
> Because I could not cease from sin.
> The more I strove against its pow'r,
> I sinn'd and stumbled but the more;
> Till late I heard my Saviour say:
> Come hither, soul, for I'm the way.
> *Lo, glad I come, and thou, dear Lamb,
> Shalt take me to thee, as I am.
> Nothing but sin I thee can give,
> Yet help me and thy praise I'll live.
> I'll tell to all poor sinners round
> What a dear Saviour I have found;
> I'll point to thy redeeming blood
> And say, behold the way to God.

The stanzas marked with an asterisk have fallen into disuse.

Cennick contributed also a score or more dialogues as the title of his collection indicated. These were antiphonal pieces, used in the dissenters' gatherings where the women sat on one side of the meeting house and the men on the other and sang back and forth. Cennick gave the men the initiative:

> Tell us, O women! we would know
> Whither so fast ye move.

to which the women responded:

> We're call'd to leave the world below,
> Are seeking one above.

Or the men would sing:

> We thank the Lamb that ye we meet
> Ye women travelling here,
> Ye fellow pilgrims, well we greet,
> And glad ye persevere.

or

> Damsels, arise, and ye who chuse
> To marry with the Lamb;
> We other lovers hence refuse
> And all beside disdain.

This last was "for the feast of charity," afterwards called the "love feast."[10] The dialogue style remained popular for perhaps a hundred years or until women got their right to sit beside their men and when thus the whole point to this musically and religiously sublimated group flirtation was lost.

Cennick also provided a number of hymns for special occasions: parting with a minister, receiving again a minister, the death of a husband and comfort for his widow, comfort to all who mourned "like the lonesome dove." All

---

10 The religious song in dialogue form was no new thing in the British Isles in Cennick's time. A number of songs in this form are to be found in the *Gude and Godlie Ballatis* of nearly two hundred years before. There they seem to have been inspired by and to some extent translated from the German. See for example the first stanzas of the "dyaloge," "Ane sang of the flesche and the spirit" and its German antecedent "Von dem streyte des fleisches wider den geyst" (Mitchell reprint, pp. 26 and 246).

Ane sang	**Von dem streyte**
All Christin men tak tent and leir,	Nun horend zu, ihr Christen leüt,
How Saull and body ar at weir;	wie leyb und seel ghenander streyt:
Upone this eird, baith lait and air,	Allhie auff erd in dieser zeit
With cruell battell Identile,	hand sie ein statigs kriegen,
And ane may nocht ane wyther flé	kains mag vom andern fliehen.

these are early appearances—the earliest we know in the religious movement under scrutiny—of patterns which reappear in the country song of America during the following century and more.

Another contemporary hymnster joined with Cennick in furnishing new songs for *Sacred Hymns*,—his still younger co-worker Joseph Humphreys (*b.* 1720). To him we are indebted for the ballad *Thanksgiving for the Progress of the Gospel in Various Parts of the World*. In these stanzas, which give a sort of map of the Great Awakening, he tells of the few preachers of the Whitefieldian-Edwardean brand who

> .... wander up and down
> To the poor blind world unknown,

but whose work is prospering.

> Souls in Europe, not a few
> Find the Gospel-tidings true.
> Britain's Isle has catch'd the flame,
> Many know and love the Lamb.
> Both in England and in Wales,
> And in Scotland grace prevails.
> London, Wilts, and Glou'stershire
> Feel our Saviour very dear.
> Bristol sinners seek the Lord,
> And in Kingswood[11] he's ador'd.
> And our Shepherd's arm enfolds
> Edinburgh and Glasgow souls.
> Muthel, Kilslith, Cambuslang,[12]

---

11   Kingswood was Whitefield's headquarters.

12   In 1742 Cambuslang, Lanarkshire, Scotland, was the scene of a great revival excitement. The local preacher, a man of decidedly Whitefieldian bent, brought his hearers to the crying, hand-clapping, breast-beating, shaking, trembling, fainting, convulsing point—according to Rees' *Cyclopaedia*, article on "Imitation."

Late of Jesus' love have sang.
Many Germans walk with God,
Through the virtue of Christ's blood.
Likewise in America (pronounced Amerikay)
Shines the glorious Gospel-day.
Fair it rises to our sight;
Jesus, make it thy delight.
Pensylvania (sic) has been blest
With an Evangelick feast.
On South Carolina too
Christ distills his heav'nly dew.
Lord be praisèd for thy work
In the Jersey's[13] and New York;
And in every other place
Where appears the Saviour's grace.
O defend the Orphan-house;[14]
Lo, it stands amidst its foes.
Hear our cries, the children bless,
Father of the fatherless.
Thousand Negroes praise thy name,
And New England's in a flame.
Triumphs in thy Mercy's power;
Jesus, call ten thousand more!
And we hear the Hottentot
By our Lord is not forgot;
And that Greenland's frozen soil
Now's become his crosses spoil.

In Humphreys' familiarity with religious doings of the dissenters in America we see signs of a community of endeavor between workers in Britain and those on this side of the Atlantic. Was there also a give and take in song? Did folky songs like Cennick's and Humphreys' come across the

---

13 Should read: the Jerseys. The territory of the present New Jersey was then divided into East and West Jersey.

14 The Orphan-house was founded by George Whitefield in Savannah, Georgia, in 1740, with money raised in England and the colonies.

water? If so, when? What signs are there of it?

Whitefield did little or nothing during his many and extended sojourns here to introduce or to spread song. He really didn't need songs very badly. A powerful Boanerges himself, he was able to arouse his hearers, merely by his hellfire preaching, to the high pitch of emotion necessary for their conversion. His lone-itinerant program, too, militated against song propaganda. It excluded from use all but those songs his far separated crowds could readily sing from memory. And those were undoubtedly merely the psalms. It is significant that Whitefield did not even feel the need of a hymn book of his own editing before 1753, after he had roamed the colonies off and on for twenty years. It is also noteworthy that with all the Whitefieldian rage in this country his *Hymns*—with their Watts and Wesley backlogs and their Cennick kindling wood—waited until 1765 for their first American printing. From this we might well guess that these sorts of hymns may have been sung here to some small extent before the Revolution. But whether they were then sung to actual folk melodies, as they certainly were later, is anybody's guess.

In the foregoing paragraphs we have presented all the obtainable data as to the appearance of folk-like song in the dissenters' flare-up in Britain and the colonies during the forty-odd years preceding the Revolution. The findings have certainly been meager. The period must, in view of this, be looked on as one in which a folk-religious movement was still without a suitable and satisfying body of song; this being due (1) to the lack of interest or/and bad judgment of those who set themselves up as leaders and (2) to the fact that it had not yet occurred to the far scattered dissenters generally that they could use their own traditional folk melodies as the setting for spiritual texts.

A Free Folk Takes Religion in Hand

> Rights of conscience in these days
> Now demand our solemn praise;
> Here we see what God has done
> By his servant, Washington.
> —Shaker *Millennial Praises*, 1813, p. 281

In depicting for ourselves the conditions which led to the Revolutionary War we should give greater prominence, I believe, to the long-drawn-out internal struggle of the variously dispossessed backwoods people against the tidewater Tory magistrates and landlords; thus also of the religious outcasts of the land against their American religious oppressors in the Established and Standing framework. And in the winning of the war and in the consolidating of its gains we should, I feel, give more generous credit to those same backwoodsmen, the bulk of the fighters, to their dissentist religious leaders of whom we have spoken and to their more or less likeminded political leaders, the Patrick Henrys, Thomas Jeffersons, and James Monroes as well as to George Washington. But however we may view it, the war was won and the insurgent yeomen gained at least some of the freedom for which they had fought; notably the freedom to worship God according to the dictates of their own conscience, a *dissenter freedom*.

The significance of this achievement is, I believe, generally underestimated. It assumes greater historical meaning, perhaps, if we recall that *it was the first instance in Christendom that a folk had won full liberty in the religious phase of its culture*, freedom not only from the coercions of magistrates, princes, kings and emperors, but also from any and all religious institutional constraints. This meant more than we can easily conceive to the millions of descendants of those Old World dissenters who had carried on their struggle for centuries against religious regimentation and persecution by meeting secretly in catacombs, caves, garrets, kitchens, cellars, conventicles, and in the woods. Now their persecutions and fears of persecution were ended. Yorktown forecast the doom of authoritative religious institutions in the United States and the Bill of Rights, 1784, sealed it.

The standing institutions did not disappear suddenly, of course. They have not disappeared yet. But their power over unwilling masses was gone. The real stature of the revulsion against them is shown by the census of a hundred years later, 1890, which gave the combined memberships of Congregational and Anglican (Episcopal) Churches as but one-fourteenth of those of all American Protestant denominations, and as but one-twentieth of American church members of all faiths, a ratio which probably holds also for the present time.

But what did the masses do with the freedom which was suddenly theirs? Americans could now worship God in a manner dictated by their conscience. But conscience—what is conscience? Did they know? They must have felt it as a strictly individual affair. And how may one be sure of what it dictates? That's another hard one! These were nice sounding words, but how could they be translated into reality? "Freedom from legislated religious restrictions" was real, concrete enough. The rest was abstract, fluid; and fluids refuse to take on forms. Consciences, dictates and manners in religious affairs were potentially as numerous

Old School Baptist Church, Hopewell, New Jersey. Built 1747, rebuilt 1822. From a photograph of the 1880s or earlier. Monument at right is to John Hart (1707–1780), member of the church and signer of the Declaration of Independence. The Old Baptists of Hopewell have sung folk-hymns ever since they gave up the psalm-tune tradition. They are singing them still.

BAPTISTS FOUGHT FOR FREEDOM. STANDING ON THIS BLOCK at the close of the service in the church shown opposite, on Sunday, April 23, 1775, Joab Haughton "inspired the men with love of liberty and desire for independence. In closing he said: 'Men of New Jersey, they are murdering your brethren of New England (Battle of Lexington)! Who follows me to Boston?' Every man answered 'I.'"—From inscription on the foundation made when the block was re-erected near John Hart's grave, July 4, 1896. Photograph by Savidge, Hopewell, New Jersey.

as the people involved in following conscience dictates and in devising worship manners. To make religious matters worse, the removal of all compulsions encouraged the growth also of those masses opposed to *all* religious methods of worship—to religion as such. Those were times, as we have mentioned, of freedom not only *of* and *in* religion, but also *from* it. (It will be remembered that Rationalism was still rampant; that Thomas Paine, the noted atheist, was also a staunch supporter of the American Revolution; and that Washington, Jefferson, Randolph of Roanoke, and Madison were quite deistic.) These disintegrating factors brought about a post-war condition which was quite chaotic, anarchic, at least from the viewpoint of institutionalized religion.

It is hard to understand chaos. But, in my determination to learn more about this chaos, I went to the church-denominational historians. There I found everything seemingly serene. My hypothesis of institutional chaos *seemed* to be a false one. The seeming serenity is illustrated for example by the chroniclers' figures for growth of the Baptists.

At the time of the Revolution, Baptists were more numerous than the members of any other sect which was not "standing" or "established." From then on they bred astoundingly fast, doubling their Revolutionary War size (if we may believe Asplund's membership lists) three to four times before the next century got under way.[15] While

---

15   Scattered data on the exceptional growth period: From 1740 to 1790 the Baptists in New England grew from twenty-one feeble churches to 226 with 17,174 members. Most of this growth was in the backwoods and after 1768 (A. H. Newman, *A History of the Baptist Churches in the United States*, New York, 1894, p. 271).

In the New York district, largely upstate, the 4,000 Baptists of 1792 had increased to 18,500 by 1812 (*Ibid.*, p. 283).

The New Jersey, Pennsylvania and Delaware Baptists were of the conservative sort. There were in 1762 only forty-two churches of them with 3,000 members (*Ibid.*, p. 272ff); and these grew only

the Baptist figures show fast growth, they must be interpreted; we must examine them closely for their great ingredient of rebellion—a subject distasteful to most denominationally loyal chroniclers. Just a word as to intra-Baptist separatism.

Baptists, while traditionally beyond the pale—in Europe, British Isles and the American colonies—were now endured and in some places had already become rather static, respectable and civilized, as they were for example in Rhode Island and New Jersey. The New England and southern backlands, on the other hand, were the stamping ground of the fractious. In the northeast these hinterland Baptists took on such names as "New Light" and "Free Will" Baptists and in the south they were the "Separates," while the fewer intransigents were called "Regulars."

The rebellious Baptists had a number of grouches. Chief among these was their conviction (then becoming

---

to the modest figure of about 4,000 in the following nine years according to Asplund.

The 5,000 members in Virginia in 1774 (William T. Thom, *The Struggle for Religious Freedom in Virginia*, Baltimore, 1900, p. 30) had become a group of 15,000 in ten years and 20,000 by 1792 (*Ibid.*, p. 303).

Asplund's figures of Baptist membership by states in 1791 are:

Vermont	1,610	Delaware	409
New Hampshire	1,732	Maryland	776
Massachusetts	7,116	Virginia	20,443
Connecticut	3,194	North Carolina	884
Rhode Island	3,512	South Carolina	4,167
New York	3,987	Georgia	3,211
New Jersey	2,279	District of "Kentucke"	7,503
Pennsylvania	1,260		

These communicants were in 868 churches with 1,132 ministers. This information is from "John Asplund, a Sweed," as he signed himself, *The Annual Register of the Baptist Denomination in North America to the First of November, 1790*. Preface signed in Southampton County, Virginia, 1791.

widespread also in other groups as we shall presently see) that the "Particular" Baptists' belief that certain humans were predestined to go to heaven and that the rest were slated for hell—just wasn't true. Parallel to their tenet that one man was as good as another and should enjoy the same rights in mundane democratic life, ran the other belief that all were the same before God and should and did enjoy the same chances of eternal life. They made their Bible tell them this. Grace was free. The human will was free to accept grace. The bringing of this message to mankind was their chief mission. Thus while the Particular (Regular) Baptists (Presbyterians and Congregationalists as well) still faced the dead-end of "election," the variously labeled Arminian or rebel Baptists looked down the broad road of revivalism. They traveled this road and grew by leaps and bounds. In them was the spirit of the times.

Other minor divisive questions concerned the preachers' call as against ministerial education and ordination, plain clothes for preachers against clerical vestments, and so on and on. They were small matters as we view them, but big enough then to divide Baptists from other Baptists.

An early leader of the northeastern Baptist schismatics was Benjamin Randall, tailor and self-made preacher born in New Castle, New Hampshire, 1749.[16] He kindled the Free Will fires in 1780.[17] For ten years the conflagration flamed high in Maine, New Hampshire and Vermont with human fuel from Regular Baptists, from the Whitefieldian New Lights, from those who couldn't

---

16 He was twenty-one when George Whitefield, making his last round, came to Portsmouth. Whitefield was much opposed as "a vagrant fanatic." At first Randall, too, was violently antagonistic to him. But he listened to him for a week. On the following Sunday Whitefield died in Newburyport. Randall repented. (See Stewart, *op. cit.*, p. 34ff.)

17 In this he may have been helped by "The Dark Day" on May 19 of that year.

tolerate the more urban Congregationalists and from the ranks of just plain "poor sinners."[18]

Just as the ranks of the stand-patting Baptists had been thinned by the Free Will schism, so also were the Free Will folk soon (1784 on) to be the victims of a similar flop-over among its churches to the Shakers. Edward Lock and his Canterbury, New Hampshire, Free Will flock were the first to be "drawn into the Shaker whirlpool." Strafford, New Hampshire, was the next. Thence Shakerism attacked the Maine churches; the "unstable" folk everywhere being easily "deluded" by the new and "fanatical notions of worship" until there was "not one of the free churches but suffered from their (the Shakers') proselyting effects."[19]

The New England picture is thus a confused one. It is quite difficult to isolate those called Shakers, Shaking Quakers, New Lighters, Free Baptists, Dancing Baptists, Randallites, Open Communionists and Free Willers one from the other; and it would be futile to expect any classification one might make to hold from year to year and from place to place. It would be comparatively easy, on the other hand, for the sociologists and psychologists to find in them all a mass-emotional common denominator, perhaps the one I have suggested above, the emotional excesses of a folk long oppressed having its first fling at freedom. It would be correct, too, I believe, to look on the groups named above as precursors emotionally of the ecstatic groups which are now spoken of loosely as Holy

---

18 By 1790 the Free Willers had twenty churches, mostly in Maine. (This may explain the complete absence of Maine data from Asplund's Baptist state-by-state membership statistics for 1791.) By 1799 they had gained thirty-three more congregations, in a territory which crept across New Hampshire into Vermont; and by 1809 sixty-nine more churches had been added to their list in these three states.

19 According to Stewart, *op. cit.*, p. 66f.

Rollers,—groups which, incidentally, are still to be found in New England as elsewhere.

I have called attention to the south as another Baptist hotbed with almost two-thirds of all American Baptists there at the end of the eighteenth century. The Virginia Separate Baptist fires mounted highest. They were fed by wandering down-east preachers of free grace and users of the revival for swelling their ranks. The 15,000 members in Virginia in 1784 grew to 20,000 in 1790 and more than 35,000 by 1812. This despite the epidemic of wanderlust which raged in their ranks and took many thousands of them, sometimes by whole congregations, into the new land of Kentucky.[20] The 7,500 Baptists in the District of Kentucky in 1791 as listed by Asplund grew by 1809 to 31,000 and helped that sect to hold its lead there over all others.

We should remind the reader here again, just to be sure of the record, that those we have been discussing were by and large the rebellious Baptists,—Free Will, Separate, etc. These were the transient Baptists that grew, spread, became variegated and, in time and in part, modern and standardized. On the other hand, the Particular, Regular, predestinarian Baptists and some subdivisions subsequently called Primitive and Old-School Baptists remained intransigent and waned as do all institutions unwilling to go along with the times.

Along with the post-Revolutionary Baptist boom came another movement—the march of the Methodists. The Baptists had a long head start over the Methodists

---

20 David Benedict (*A General History of the Baptist Denomination in America*, Boston, 1913, ii, p. 92ff) tells of the early civilizing of the Virginia Baptists after the fires of the 1785 revival went out; how the wild ones had migrated in a body to Kentucky, the stay-at-homes had become decent, and "odd tones, disgusting whoops and awkward gestures were disused." — This looks like wishful chronicling.

everywhere in the land and they maintained this lead more or less evenly for a number of decades. Their new Wesleyan competitors, with the same free-grace and revival equipment, had hardly made a good start in the New York to Virginia region before they were badly hampered and their activities interrupted by the Revolution against Britain, the headquarters of all the early Methodist missionaries. Despite this enforced interruption there were between four and five thousand members of this new sect at the close of the war, a number which grew before the end of the century to the surprisingly big total of 60,000, most of them in the south,—whites and blacks being in the ratio of about four to one.

The New England Baptists missionized, as we have seen, largely in the south. The southern Methodists, as they grew in strength, missionized in New England,— an interesting anomaly in such activity. For a long time, however, the results of the Wesleyans' doings in darkest down-east were disappointing. The still influential Congregationalists would have no traffic with these Methodists who had "come up from the south—a set of broken merchants who, having become poor and being too lazy to work, had taken this method of preaching to procure a livelihood."[21] It was also their free-grace doctrine that the Calvinistic Congregationalists didn't like.

In the New England back country the Methodists' revivals and Gospel would have gone over better had the country Yankees not already satisfied their souls' longings with other rampant folk-religious movements, those of which we have already spoken. With most of the fuel thus out of the Methodists' reach their down-east fires could not flare high. Out of the 60,000 American Methodists at the end of the eighteenth century only 3,000 were New

---

21 Nathan Bangs, *A History of the Methodist Church*. New York, ed. 1880, i, 293.

Englanders.

While the Wesleyans appeared in force on the American scene just in time to capitalize on the freedom-and-equality movement they brought along their anomalous, hierarchic organizations. This, in a land and at a time of free-roving preachers (notably Baptists) and free-shifting tenets, just wouldn't work. And before the end of the century the Methodist individualists led by James O'Kelly of Virginia deserted the Wesleyan ranks in a mass, and precisely on the issue of their objection to church control from headquarters. The schism started in 1792 in Virginia. From 1795 to 1801 regular Methodist membership figures stood still in Virginia at 14,000. We have in the O'Kelly movement then a case of the free deserting the free to become freer,—much like the Particular Baptist to Free Will Baptist to Shaker flocking in New England.

The Congregationalists suffered from the new spirit of revolt. Arminianism and Socinianism, both yoke-throwing isms, honeycombed their sect. By 1800, Harvard University and one-third of the churches in New England had gone over to these free ways of thinking, ways which were adopted variously by the Deists, Unitarians, Hicksite Quakers and Universalists.

The Presbyterians were largely in the middle colonies. The Whitefieldian excitement had split them wide open as early as 1741 into Old Side and New Side; the latter standing for (a) greater freedom in preaching itinerancy, (b) less strictness in preacher education, (c) soft-pedaling "election" and, more important than all the rest, (d) revivals and whatever "enthusiasm" (shouting and the like) went with them.

The Tenments had carried on New Sidism before the Revolution, with the Log College in New Jersey (the real grandmother of Princeton University) as their point of semination. Samuel Davies carried it later into Pennsylvania and Virginia. We shall see presently how the Presbyterians were subjected to another storm-and-stress of the same sort as a result of the Great Revival of 1800-plus.

Divisive and disintegrative in its effects on existing institutions, the dissent eruption had in time quite the opposite effect on the minds of the masses of those taking part in the movement. It tended in a sense to unite a nation that was ethnically heterogeneous. Dissenting Anglo-Saxon yeomen in the northeast; Germans, all varieties of Gaels, and other minor ethnic groups in the middle states; Gaels (notably Scotch-Irish) and French Huguenots in the south,—all had the new free-religious outlook in common. Pennsylvania Germans flocked to hear itinerant preachers whose language they couldn't even understand. Georgia French peasants became shouting Baptists. The backwoodsmen of Maine, New Hampshire, Vermont, Massachusetts and New York became not only Free Will Baptists but also, later, shouting Methodists under the spell of missioners from the south. Thus these tag-ends of uprooted and disjointed Europeans got their first experience (though hardly recognizing it, probably) in New World unity, in America-consciousness, in becoming parts of a brand new composite folk. And it was that early, as we shall see, that even the black folk, slaves as well as free, began to feel their real though comparatively humble part in the making of the nation. And all this came about through the instrumentality of religion.

Socially the new free religion was one for the common man. This has already been touched on; but it must be stressed. The common man was the poor man. Hence the religion of the poor Nazarene had, also in this respect, come back to first principles and its first aspects. Among the rebellious and now free religionists, poverty lost its stigma, was lauded even. Riches were the sinful things and were condemned. Fine clothing and other luxuries were never in greater disrepute than then and among those plain people. There were practically no schools, so "learning" became superfluous, vicious even. "Real wisdom" flowed from the Bible, from right thinking and right believing. This, it may be seen, was precisely the soil for the growth of egalitarianism.

That the folk religion struck its strongest roots into the American *rural* soil rather than that of the towns and coastal cities has been abundantly clear. Centers of population were dens of iniquity. Their churches had steeples, pews and the like—all bad. Plain windowless log meeting houses were the backwoods Americans' gathering places; and the seats were often no more than logs. The free-religionists were thus destined from the start to occupy the great stretches of the land.

The more remote from urban controls a religious movement is, the more it tends to go wild. The American country religious developments of the post-Revolutionary generation under discussion were no exception to this rule. Religious wildness in America has been documented from the Edwardean revivals of the 1730s on to those more than a hundred years after. Among Evangelicals, off-brand Baptists, Methodists or what you will, the picture of mass hysteria was the same, varying only in intensity from time to time and place to place. The preacher, as we saw in Chapter I, was always the chief inducer of the hysteria. At its mildest it took the form of weeping. At its wildest its victims went temporarily or even permanently insane.[22] In between, all the degrees.

---

22   Scattered data in addition to those given in Chapter I:

Jonathan Edwards (New England pre-Whitefieldian revivalist) got his hearers to fainting, falling, going into trances, convulsing, crying out; "some even lost their reason." (Davidson, p. 183)

At a Maine coast baptism of forty-one people in the 1790s the

We must bear in mind that the one religious conviction running through this whole movement was that all institutional mediacy between man's soul and its Redeemer must be rejected. These "deluded" masses were thus the possessors of a live *personal* faith, the livers of a vigorous *inner* Christianity, real pietists without that concomitant of quietism which had been forced on their European religious forebears; real mass insisters that "religious freedom" should mean just what it says.

The movement did not end with the eighteenth century. It did not even reach its climax within that period. Before following it further, however, we shall give some space to the consideration of the song aspects from Revolutionary times—where we dropped the matter at the end of Chapter II—through the first three decades of the nineteenth century.

---

saved cried "Glory!" "Old saints responded ... and, mingled with these were the cries of wounded sinners, so that the noise was heard afar off." (Stewart, p. 138)

The parish preacher in Brunswick, Maine, wouldn't let Benjamin Randall, founder of Free Will Baptists, into his pulpit, didn't like the "excitement among his people." So Randall preached in the evening at a deacon's home where "sinners cried for mercy and saints shouted for joy" until three in the morning. (Stewart, p. 71)

"Separates" (who broke away from the Particular Baptists of New Jersey and Pennsylvania and further south just as the Free Willers had in the northeast) were "very noisy," jerked, barked, rolled, and leaped as early as the revival of 1785–1792 in Virginia, according to Thom, p. 17. *Cf.* also Sweet, p. 11, and Bennett, p. 38.

In the Carolinas the Boston Baptist Boanerges, Shubael Stearns, caused "trembling, weeping, screaming, catalepsy" notably at Sandy Creek Church, Guilford County, North Carolina. (Newman, p. 293)

Freedom in Religion Begets Freedom in Singing. Religious Folk Song is Born.

> My theme to preach, my song to sing
> My only joy till death—Amen!

The work of the few powerfully preaching "Gospel Trumpeters" like Edwards, Whitefield, the Tennents and others was soon taken over, as we have seen, by the numerous Gospel tin-horn tooters. These were zealous and noisy converts who went at once to exhorting, preaching, telling everybody what the Lord had done for their souls, but not much else. As cogent religious persuasion receded, stark emotionalism and hellfire took its place; and the need for song as an emotion-augmentative became pressing.

We have seen however that there was little song at hand,—at least, song of the sort that the new American folk-religious conditions demanded. So the folk saw they would have to take the matter into their own hands and make their songs, just as they had taken the other phases of worship into their own hands and were busy recasting them. And that is precisely what they went about doing. They made lyrics of all sorts and adopted for them the general name of "hymns and spiritual songs," a title which tended to distinguish them from the older psalms. I shall consider in this chapter the texts alone.

All we know about the texts is what we read in the little tuneless hymn and spiritual-song booklets of the period; at first almost exclusively those of the Baptists and their offshoots. These books were compiled in most cases by or for wandering revivalist preachers and were printed wherever the wanderer happened to be tarrying a while. There were scores of these compilations. A few had wide and long usefulness.

As typical of the country-Baptist song-book trend let us look first at Joshua Smith's *Divine Hymns or Spiritual Songs*. The American revolt against Britain had been over but three years when Smith, a New Hampshire layman, had a Norwich, Connecticut, printshop do his book.[23] Its songs were flat on the folk level, reflecting all the new, free, country-individualistic Baptist and New Light religious trends,—free grace, believers' baptism and all that. The book's usefulness is proved by its at least eleven editions during the nineteen years between 1784 and 1803. And its spread is indicated by the towns where some of these editions came out: Portsmouth, New Hampshire, 1794; Elizabethtown, (state unknown), 1800; Exeter, New Hampshire, 1801; Wilkes-Barre, Pennsylvania, 1802; and Portland, Maine, 1803. Three editions at least appeared in Norwich, Connecticut. In the Portland edition Smith's name as editor was joined with that of Samuel Sleeper. Even though *Divine Hymns* had—in its 1803 edition at least—only 142 small pages of texts, 197 hymns, thirty-seven of them were country stand-bys (Watts and more nearly contemporary hymn writers) which bore the stamp of folk approval then and subsequently. Practically all the rest were of the homespun sort and not long-lived.

As *Divine Hymns* was running its course and running

---

23 Cf. Louis F. Benson. *The English Hymn, Its Development and Use.* Philadelphia, 1915, p. 202.

out, another Smith and a Jones carried on the country-hymn propaganda. Elias Smith and Abner Jones were at first Baptists of the rebellious Free Will sort. Their convictions as to religious independence drove them both to desert (quite independently of each other) even that free sect. They met accidentally and started co-operatively a religious group which they called "Christians." First Elias Smith compiled *Hymns for the Use of Christians*, Boston, 1804. Jones' collection was *The Melody of the Heart*, same town, same year. Then the two worked together and produced a year later another compilation under a variant of Smith's title, *Hymns, Original and Selected, for the Use of Christians*, Boston, 1805.

It is from these and other similar booklets that we get our clearest picture of post-Revolutionary country singing. I present the picture in two parts, that is, (a) with a list of opening lines of the sturdy old texts which entered the American country song tradition during the post-Revolutionary period or earlier and rooted there, and (b) with a series of citations from other contemporary hymn texts, for various reasons shorter lived, but revealing some of the many colors appearing in and characterizing the folk singing in the religious atmosphere of rural America in those very years.

The list of the older hymns which were then popular and have proved lasting follows.

Ah, where am I now? when was it or how
Ah, woe is me, constrained to dwell among the sons of night
Afflictions, though they seem severe – *Newton*
Alas, and did my Saviour bleed – *Watts*
All glory and praise to the Ancient of days (sung to the 'Old
    German' tune)
Almighty love inspires my heart with sacred fire
Amazing grace, how sweet the sound—*Newton*
Arise, my dear love my undefiled dove—*Holden*

Immersion at the "Baptisterion" about a mile and a half out of Philadelphia around the middle of the eighteenth century. To the Helmsey tune they sang the following song:

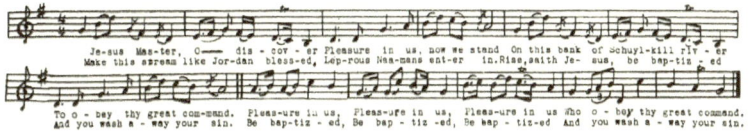

Picture and print from Morgan Edwards' *Materials Towards A History of the Baptists in Pennsylvania*, two vols., Philadelphia, 1770 and 1792, frontispiece and p. 129f.

As on the cross the Saviour hung and wept and bled and died—*Stennett*
Attend, ye saints, and hear me tell (a typical "experience" song)
Begone, unbelief, my Saviour is near—*Newton*
Behold the Savior of mankind—*Samuel Wesley, Sr.*
Beside the gospel pool appointed for the poor—*Newton*
Broad is the road that leads to death—*Watts*
By the poor widow's oil—*Newton*
Children of the heavenly king—*Cennick*
Christ he sits on Zion's hill
Come all that are New Lights indeed
Come all ye dear souls who are of Adam's loin
Come all ye mourning (wandering) pilgrims dear
Come all ye poor sinners that from Adam came (A 'Lazarus' ballad)
Come and taste along with me consolation running free
Come brothers and sisters that love my dear Lord
Come friends and relations, let's join heart and hand
Come, sinner, to the gospel feast—*Wesley*
Come thou fount of every blessing—*Robinson*
Come we (ye) that love the Lord indeed
Come ye sinners, poor and needy—*Hart*
Dismiss us with thy blessing, Lord—*Hart*
Encouraged by thy word of promise to the poor—*Newton*
Enlisted in the cause of sin, How can a good be evil
Farewell, my dear brethren, the time is at hand
Farewell, my dear brethren in the Lord
From whence doth this union arise—*Baldwin*
Glorious things of thee are spoken—*Newton*
Grace, 'tis a charming sound, harmonious to the ear—*Doddridge*
Guide me, O thou great Jehovah—*Williams*
Hail, sovereign love, that first began—*Brewer*
Hark, my soul, it is the Lord—*Cowper*
Hark how the gospel trumpet sounds
He comes, he comes, the Judge severe—*Wesley*
He dies, the friend of sinners dies—*Watts*
How can I sleep while angels sing
How firm a foundation, ye saints of the Lord—*Keen*

How tedious and tasteless the hours—*Newton*
How sweet the name of Jesus sounds
I'm not ashamed to own my Lord—*Watts*
In evil long I took delight—*Newton*
I set myself against the Lord
I would but cannot sing—*Newton*
Jesus, and shall it ever be—*Grigg*
Jesus, my all, to heaven is gone—*Cennick*
Let Christ, the glorious lover
Life is the time to serve the Lord—*Watts*
Let party names no more the Christian world
    o'erspread—*Beddome*
Lo, he comes with clouds descending
Lord, dismiss us with thy blessing—*Fawcett*
Mercy, O thou Son of David—*Newton*
My days, my weeks, my months, my years
My load of sin is gone
Now the Savior stands a-pleading
Of him who did salvation bring
O for a closer walk with God—*Cowper*
O for a glance of heavenly day—*Hart*
O happy souls, how fast you move
O Jesus my Savior, I know thou art mine
(O) now begin the heavenly theme—*Langford*
O may I worthy prove to see the saints in full prosperity
O thou in whose presence my soul takes delight—*Swain*
Physician of my sin-sick soul—*Hart*
Remember, sinful youth, you must die, you must die
Salvation, O the joyful sound—*Doddridge*
Savior, I do feel thy merit
Savior, visit thy plantation—*Newton*
Sometimes a light surprizes the Christian while he
    sings—*Cowper*
Stop, poor sinner, stop and think—*Newton*
That awful day will surely come—*Watts*
That glorious day is drawing nigh
That great tremendous day's approaching
The day is past and gone, the evening shades appear—*Leland*
The fields are all white

FREEDOM IN RELIGION BEGETS FREEDOM IN SINGING.

The great God of love
The Lord into his garden comes
The voice of free grace—*Heber*
There is a fountain filled with blood—*Cowper*
The time is soon coming, by prophets foretold
Though troubles assail and dangers affright (*The Lord Will
    Provide*)—*Newton*
'Tis a point I long to know—*Newton*
Throughout our Savior's life we trace
We've found the Rock, the travelers cried
When converts first begin to sing
When Joseph his brethren beheld—*Newton*

This is really a very excellent batch of hymns. Not all of them appeared in every booklet of the period; but each appeared in many, and most of them appeared *only* in the country collections. They are not the work of those called "great religious poets." They sum up rather as a folk-selected anthology from the pens of two to three generations of intensely and emotionally religious youth, dissenters all. The largest contribution, seventeen, to the 53 authored hymns in the list was made by that two-year-schooled, "godless sailor," navy deserter, slave ship captain John Newton. Converted and a Whitefield-Wesleyan dissenter in his twenties, he became a hymn writer and preacher in his thirties. Most of his hymns in the above list picture vividly his own soul struggles; hence their lasting appeal to those in similar throes.[24] They became available to

---

24 Not only were Newton's heart and soul in the right place, he also had a clear idea of what he was doing. Watts, he declared rightly in his preface to the *Olney Hymns*, worked hard to "restrain his (poetic) fire, and to accommodate himself to the capacities of common readers." Whereas he (Newton) did his best to attain "a stile (*sic*) ... suited to the composition of hymns," an attainment easier for "a versifier (Newton himself) than a poet." "They should be *hymns, not odes*, if designed for public worship and for the use of plain people. Perspicuity, simplicity and ease should be chiefly attended to; and the imagery and coloring of poetry, if

American compilers and singers only slowly through the English *Olney Hymns* in which most of his and Cowper's work appeared in 1779.

At first glance, the eminent Dr. Isaac Watts might seem to be an exception to the hymn-writing youth movement. But when we remember that he was still a boy in his twenties when he wrote the great mass of those hymns which eventually made the name of Watts synonymous with a long enduring "true style" in religious group-song, we realize how well he fitted into the virile youth category. The fact that but seven of Watts' hymns appear in the list means merely that he had not yet arrived (as he did later) in the American backwoods.

We have already spoken (in Chapter II) of youthful John Cennick. Joseph Grigg, who wrote the listed *Jesus, and shall it ever be'* at the tender age of ten, seems to hold the youth record. All the known authors but John Leland were Britishers.

The ninety-three hymns listed are fairly even-keeled in character. The new American religious turmoil does not appear in them. For a reflection of this new movement's real colors we must hunt in the American collections among the many scores of songs which were *not* of the old stock, were new, had not had time to become widely accepted as material for borrowing and lending from booklet to booklet, or had not yet been eliminated from all booklets as eccentric and thus, in the long run, unusable.

In the first American Baptist song book, 1766, the hymnist repeats the lines found in John Playford's *Whole Book of Psalms* (1673):

> We sing to thee whose wisdom form'd

---

admitted at all, should be indulged very sparingly." With these principles of his craftsmanship one reason becomes clear why Newton's songs sank so deep into the folk soul.

> The curious organ of the ear;

and adds

> And whilst we sing, we'll consecrate
> That too, too much profaned art.

Group singing had been a rare practice among the Baptists.[25] This hymn shows the awakening interest in an "art" that had been known to them in its psalm-tune and its secular popular-song (profaned) forms. The following song, entitled "Innocent Sounds," develops this rationalization further.

> Enlisted in the cause of sin,
> Why should a good be evil?
> Music, alas, too long has been
> Press'd to obey the devil.
> Drunken or lewd or light the lay,
> Flows to their souls' undoing,
> Widen'd and strewn with flow'rs the way,
> Down to eternal ruin.
>
> Who on the part of God will rise,
> Innocent sounds recover?
> Fly on the prey and seize the prize,
> Plunder the carnal lover?
> Strip him of ev'ry moving strain,
> Of ev'ry melting measure?
> Music in virtue's cause retain,
> Risk the holy pleasure?[26]

We shall see presently how these folk religionists carried out their music plundering forays.

---

25 *Cf.* Benson, *op. cit.*, p. 196f.

26 *Cf. Down-East Spirituals*, No. 156.

Being Baptist or near-Baptist, the booklets had numbers of hymns to be sung in connection with special observances of that sect. Immersion was provided generously with hymns. No baby baptism for them.

> Some call it baptism and think it will stand,
> A few drops of water dropt from a man's hand,
> In the face of the infant who's under the curse;
> But we find no scripture which proves it to us.

—wrote "Anna Beaman of Warren in Connecticut ... about the time she was baptized."

> Dear Christian friends, come we will go
> And search the ark with care;
> A type of Baptism you know,
> We'll search for infants there.

The rhymnster searched and found none. It took sixteen stanzas to prove the evil of infant baptism.

The hymns had to do not only with Jesus' baptism in the Jordan. The hymnists went back for symbols even to Noah's experience in the flood. The Red Sea was a symbolic immersion for the Children of Israel. So was "the water and blood" that flowed from the side of the Savior at the crucifixion; He was baptized in His own blood and tears. In Morgan Edwards' *Materials Toward a History of the Baptists in Pennsylvania* (Philadelphia, 1770, pp. 131-132) there is a hymn that was used by the Baptists at the "Baptisterion" on the banks of the Schuylkill, just beyond Philadelphia.

There were no less than seventy-three Lord's Supper hymns in the first America-printed Baptist collection of 1766. Three of them—"How Condescending and How Kind," "'Twas on That Dar' and Doleful Night," and "When I Survey the Wondrous Cross," all by Watts—are among those which have lived on.

The country Baptists of those times were largely of the foot-washing sort. This rite always followed the Lord's Supper observance. John Cennick's

> When I see thee, Lord, ...
> At supper with thy followers sit
> And see thee wash their dirty feet.

went a bit too far in its realism to be preserved in connection with the rite. The Shakers of New Lebanon, New York, sang:

> Obedient to our Lord's commands,
> We now together meet;
> With humble hearts and cleansèd hands,
> To wash each other's feet.

A song for the same observance in the early Georgia Primitive Baptist tradition is:

> Did Christ the great example lead
> For all his humble train,
> In washing the disciples' feet
> And wiping them again?
> And did my Lord and Master say,
> "If I have wash'd your feet,
> Ye also ought to watch and pray
> And wash each other's feet?"

Weddings were provided with appropriate hymns. A good example is the song by John Berridge (1776–1793):

> Since Jesus freely did appear
> To grace the marriage feast,
> O Lord, we ask thy presence here
> To make a wedding guest.

Funerals, too, were occasions for song making, singing, exhortation and conversion,—as they still are today among the intransigent blacks of the South. The widowers sang oftenest and longest. Truman Beman, for example, "elder of the Baptist Church of Christ at Rensselaerville and Bern, composed (the following song) to be sung at the burial of his third wife, April 8, 1802," according to Miss Harvey, p. 70.

> Ye pilgrims, whilst you tarry here,
> Hear my complaint and drop a tear.
> My heart is overcome with grief;
> Where shall I go to find relief?
>
> Three wives I've had, but all are gone,
> And I am left to weep and moan.
> Nine children have been born to me,
> But four are in eternity.
>
> Three sorts of children with me left,
> Of their three mothers all bereft.
> O! the sad trial makes me weep
> And hold my waking eyes from sleep.
>
> I'd flee into the desert wild,
> Unknown to parents, wife or child.
> And dwell within some lonely cave,
> If I could find a peaceful grave.

This is less than half his recorded trouble-tale. Another bereaved husband could not express his grief in less than twenty-three stanzas. He started his lament even before his Esther died of consumption.

> My bride, the dear wife of my youth,
> Lies panting and gasping for breath.
>
> "Farewell, my dear husband," saith she,
> "Now from your kind bosom I'll leap,
> With Jesus, my bridegroom to be,
> My flesh in the tomb for to sleep."
>
> And shall I indulge my complaint,

And tell you how lonesome my bed?

Not all that gay heathens can paint
Can tell how true lovers do part.

A widow laments somewhat more briefly, hence more convincingly, beginning thus:

My head and stay is took away,
And I am left alone;
My husband dear, which was so near,
Is took away and gone.[27]

Humility was preached and sung. The faithful were mere worms, dying worms and even "panting" worms.

Dear friend of friendless sinners, hear,
And magnify thy grace divine.
Pardon a worm that would draw near,
That would his heart to thee resign,
A worm by self and sin opprest,
That pants to reach thy promis'd rest.

It was natural that the religion of the Despised and Rejected One should stress, long before its institutions and adherents had become materially rich, the most abject phases of indigence.

Throughout our Savior's life we trace
Nothing but shame and deep disgrace.

The Lazarus story and that of the Prodigal Son were

---

27 Peak's *Baptist Hymns and Spiritual Songs*, Windsor, (New Hampshire?), 1793, p. 15. H. M. Belden published in his *Missouri Ballads and Songs*, 1940, p. 467, a close variant of five stanzas of this six-stanza song as it was furnished him from a Civil War diary. In the first line of his manuscript text "My head and stay is loof away" the word "loof" perplexed him. The above song of 70 years before shows the word to have been probably merely a hand-writing error for "took."

sung in numbers of versions. Newton's "Beggar's Prayer" was a favorite:

> Encourag'd by thy word of promise to the poor,
> Behold a beggar, Lord, waits at thy mercy-door.
> I have no right to say that though I now am poor,
> Yet once there was a day when I possessèd more.

and so on for eight stanzas ending in

> Such pleas are mine men would not hear,
> But God receives a beggar's prayer.

The poor and humble were to have their reward above. The opposite got hell. It took thirty-seven stanzas in Miss Harvey's Yankee Baptist hymn book to list the many brands of sinners and to check them off on an imaginary Judgment Day.

> Hark, from the skies what's this I hear?
> A loud and dreadful sound!

Then she stands aside and notes the types on the downward road: hypocrites, Pharisees, the profane, Sunday profaners, scoffers, adulterers, foolish virgins, fornicators, "sottish, drunken, base, vile souls," the sordid, distracting souls, backbiters, liars all, "executioners, oppressors too"; and Topheth is prepared for those

> Who basely and who cruelly
> Devour the helpless poor.

Elder Elias Smith delivered a lyric "address to young Person at a window" presumably in the Boston red-light district.

> When your rosy cheeks are pale,
> When your sparkling eyes go blind,
> You must leave this mournful vale,
> And your sinful joys behind.

FREEDOM IN RELIGION BEGETS FREEDOM IN SINGING.

Sinful joys in the form of dancing to which its proponents gave the innocent name of "civil mirth" came in for its big share of Baptist condemnation. A converted female confesses:

> The darling sin I did commit
> Was that which some delight in yet:
> That heinous sin call'd civil mirth
> God threatens with his dreadful wrath.
>
> At length I heard a Baptist preach;
> His words quite thru my heart did reach.
> He said I must be born again
> If ever heav'n I would obtain.

For all this fun abstracted from man's daily life, compensation was pictured. For those who controlled their sex desires there was "Christ, the glorious lover" who

> ... comes to wretched sinners
> To woo himself a bride.
> She bolts the door upon him
> And bids the Lord depart;
> She will not serve his honor
> Nor let him have her heart.
>
> Yet Jesus loves the sinner
> And will not leave the door,
> But cries, "O wretched creature,
> Reject my grace no more.
> Behold my matchless fullness!
> Arise and let me in;
> How can you be so cruel
> To bar your heart with sin?
> If calls and invitation
> Will not excite your love,
> Prepare for condemnation,
> For I will not remove."

After some stanzas of threatening on the part of the

Lover the sinner-bride-elect gives in.

> The marriage is made ready,
> The parties are agreed,
> The holy son of David
> And Adam's wretched seed.
>
> They eat and drink together
> And mutually embrace.

and they live happily ever after:

> This Union shall continue
> Forevermore the same,
> And nothing part asunder
> The Christian and the Lamb.

The theme is hoary. It is closely related to biblical romances like the Song of Solomon. It appeared in the fifteenth century song:

> "What schall I [Christ] do with my fair spouse,
> But abide her of my gentilness,
> Till that sche loke out of her house
> Of fleischly affeccioun? Love mine sche is.
> Her bed is made, her bolster is bliss,
> Her chaumber is chosen; is there none mo?
> Loke out on me at the window of kindness,
> *Quia amore langueo.*"

(From *Early English Lyrics*, chosen by E. K. Chambers and F. Sidgwick, London, 1926, p. 153.) In this poem the old theme was brought up to its date and thus closer to the English folk. The unknown maker of "Glorious Lover" performed the same task for Anglo-Saxons living 300 years later.

If the poor but pious went shabby; if their hymns railed long at "gay attire which children love and fools admire" there still was comfort in contemplating that

> Dress uniform Christ's soldiers wear,
> 'Tis lined with white and faced with red,

and that, according to another variant, these uniforms are

> Not purchased by their cost or care,
> But by their Prince bestow'd.

And the well known white robes are sung:

> Those robes they wear that shine so fair
> And dazzle like the sun,
> I've kept above wrapt up in love
> And angels ne'er had one.
> Dear saints, but I was forc'd to die,
> Or you must naked gone;
> They're made for you, I know they'll do,
> For I have try'd them on.

While the chief compensation for earthly renunciation was the glorious prospect of opposite conditions in heaven, the renouncing ones seemed to get satisfaction, too, in painting the future punishment picture for those who had their fun here.

> Laugh, ye profane, and swell and burst
> With bold impiety!
> You'll go to hell
> Where devils are in black despair,
> A-burning in the fire—
> Where they must lie eternally
> And never rise no higher.
> Then shall ye curse that fatal day
> (With flames upon your tongues)
> When you exchanged your souls away

> For vanity and songs.
> You call your pleasures civil joy
> To recreate the mind;
> But soon you will your souls destroy
> As you too late will find.

Nor did even the sinner's deathbed stop their hellfire harangue:

> Ah, whence that hollow groan?
> It comes from yonder bed.
> A gasping rebel sinks oppress'd,
> His joys and hope are fled.
>
> No more with blasphemy
> His rattling throat distends;
> Forgotten now his noisy mirth
> And all his mirthful friends.

Even the Eternal One is made to join in their joy over sinners in hell:

> There through long eternity,
> They make their bed in misery,
> And shriek and nash *(sic)* their teeth, while God
> Laughs at their pain from above.
>
> The one with Dives for water cry
> And gnaw their tongues for pain;
> They gnash their teeth and parch and fry
> And wring their hands in vain.

The observer sees his own earthly Nemesis in Topheth:

> You me about the floor did drag
> And caused my soul to sin;
> And devils your souls shall gag,
> And force the fuel in.

There is a good deal of internal evidence that songs like those cited above were sung by one person—lay exhorter or zealous and musical "saint"—not by groups.

Other ballads or solo songs were of the "farewell" sort.

> Farewell, my brethren in the Lord,
> The Gospel sounds the jubilee.
> My stamm'ring tongue shall sound aloud,
> From land to land, from sea to sea.
> And as I preach from place to place,
> I trust alone in God's free grace.

Six stanzas of this, then

> My theme to preach, my song to sing,
> My only joy till death—Amen.

More folky was

> Come all my dear brethren, I bid you farewell;
> I'm going to travel to preach the Gospel.

The character of the rampant roving preacher is pictured in

> God's ministers like flames of fire
> Are passing thro' the land.
> The voice is here: "Repent and fear,
> King Jesus is at hand!"

Another popular variety of ballad was the song of religious experience, in which the saved sinner told what the Lord had done for his or her soul. This sort must have been heard often at the early Baptists' "conference" gatherings. The songs usually opened with a come-all-ye or some variant. In the Baptist collection of 1766 we read:

> O sinners, attend whilst here I relate
> The love of my friend who cancel'd my debt.

Samuel Stennett's

> Come ye that fear the Lord
> And listen while I tell
> How narrowly my feet escaped
> The snares of death and hell.

became quite at home in America. And in the probably native American

> Come all ye saints and sinners near
> Come listen a while and you shall hear.

we sense the ghost of Paul Revere.

Natural phenomena were "acts of God," as in our legal documents today, and a great help to those who would wake up sinners to the danger of their state. The earthquake of November 16, 1755, called forth a ballad-warning which Baptist Miss Harvey reprinted long after, in 1806.

> Alas! on earth how oft we spy
> Wonders descending from the sky!
>
> And the dire frighten'd trembling earth
> Abandons all her joy and mirth.
> What terrors seize on us below
> When nature speaks her overthrow!
>
> Can I with mortal tongue declare
> What horror seized the earth and air,
> When shocks from a supremer hand
> Did shake the distant wicked land?

There are nine more stanzas of narration and warning to be ready.

The Dark Day, May 19, 1780, helped bring Randall's Free Willers ("Merry Dancing Baptists") into the world and inspired the ballad from which I take the following stanzas.

FREEDOM IN RELIGION BEGETS FREEDOM IN SINGING.

1. Let us adore and bow before
   The sovreign Lord of might,
   Who turns away the shining day,
   Into the shades of night.

3. Nineteenth of May, a gloomy day,
   When darkness veil'd the sky;
   The sun's decline may be a sign
   Some great event is nigh.

17. And now let all who hear this call
    And saw the day so dark,
    Make haste away without delay
    And get into the ark.

The northern lights, too, were used.

> Behold the streaming from the north!
> Nations behold afar!
> Look to the skies with a surprize,
> He flashes through the air.
>
> The streams of light stream in the night,
> Speaks forth the day will come,
> When Christ our King his troops will bring
> And raise the dusky tomb.

(The foregoing stanzas with their medial rhyme, exemplify a pattern which had been popular for hundreds of years in English song.)

Naturally the English of these comparatively unlettered folk and/or their printers left something to be desired. We have already seen some examples. Some of their variants from today's usage however, like Watts' "Why has my God my soul forsook" and the anonymous "Nought else can e'er happify man" were allowable when written. The very first Baptist hymn book threw down the gauntlet to the tyrants of language standardization. I excerpt from here and there the following:

> Baptize 'em in the awful name.
>
> Teach 'em (in quotation marks, as the actual words of Jesus).
>
> And sink 'em (sins) so as ne'er to rise.
>
> Amazing is thy mercies, Lord.

Some further examples of English "as she was spoke and sang" in Ingalls' New Hampshire-Vermont *Christian Harmony*, 1805, are:

> Hark and hear what has befell me.
>
> I love the solemn praises
> On whom bright angels gazes.
>
> And he learns us the impartial song.

Squeamishness was not in their dictionary. Dirty feet were dirty feet to Evangelical John Cennick as we have seen. The Baptists were just as straightforward.

> See's head all torn with thorns!

and His face

> Reaking with sweat and gore!
> See his side spout a stream of blood
> And water through the wound.
>
> His sweet and reverend face
> With spittle all profan'd.

But when they sang of

> My bowels, O my bowels, I
> Am pain'd at my inmost soul.

> No, all to me is dung and dross

there was of course no physical visceral connotation.
    Peggy Dow, wife of "Crazy" Lorenzo Dow, had a hard time with her verbs.

> O had I died when I was young!
> O what would I have given.
> I might, like babes, with my little tongue
> Been praising God in heaven.

> Saith Satan: fated is your state
> Time past you might repented.

> O that I was some bird or beast,
> Was I a stork or owl,
> Some lofty tree should bear my nest,
> Or through the desert prowl.

When the hymnsters left their honest English however and ventured into Latinism they were even less sure of their way, as in

> O seek the circumcising grace,
> Be wise, do not refuse it;

(The first line of this couplet was altered in later books to read: O seek His sanctifying grace.)
    Yankee curtness is seen in:

> The time is nigh when it will do
> To have of earth six feet by two.

I cite from two hymns which bring rather unusual synonyms for Christ.

> The tree of life my soul hath seen,
> Laden with fruit and always green.

The trees of nature fruitless be,
Compared with Christ, the apple tree.[28]

A mighty Breaker sure is he,
He broke my chains and set me free.
A gracious Breaker to my soul;
He breaks and O He makes me whole.

He breaks down sin, breaks through gloomy clouds, every crafty snare, my stony heart, my pride, never His word, and for us He breaks death's cold embrace.

The above pages have been given to the textual aspects of a new spurt of singing indulged in by the new and turbulent sorts of Baptists and their religious likes up to and through the beginning of the nineteenth century. It was my original purpose to give similar treatment also to the songs of the early Methodists. I felt that if I searched their hymn books I would find folky material. I searched diligently. Found plenty of song, but it wasn't folky in any sense. I found that the Methodists had merely laid aside the dull psalm-tune tradition and taken on that which Wesley had prescribed.

As a body they had obeyed their founder's injunction to "sing no hymns of your own composing," and their American leaders' admonition: "If you have any respect for the authority of the Conference or for us or any regard for the prosperity of the Connection, ... purchase no Hymn-Books but what are signed with the names of your two Bishops" Thomas Coke and Francis Asbury.

At the turn of the century, however, signs of Methodist rebellion against this hymnodic strait-jacket appeared. The little *Spiritual Song Book* printed in Halifax, North Carolina, 1805, compiled by David B. Mintz, "Minister of the Gospel, M.E.C." (Methodist Episcopal Church),

---

28 Smith and Sleeper, 1803, p. 4. The hymn appeared first in the *London Spiritual Magazine*, August, 1761, ascribed to R.H.

and the same preacher's *Hymns and Spiritual Songs* which came out a year later in Newbern, North Carolina, contain precisely the same sorts of hymns, many of the very same folky songs indeed, which we had found in the much earlier country Baptist books of the northeast, but never before in a Methodist book.

Despite their title-page designation for the use of "the pious of all denominations," the Mintz booklets reflected the Methodist counter-offensive against the Baptists. As to baptism:

> We've searched the law of heaven,
> Throughout the sacred code;
> Of baptism there by dipping
> We've never found a word.
>
> To plunge is inconsistant (*sic*)
> Compared with holy rites;
> An instance of such business
> We've never found as yet.

John immersed Jesus to be sure. "This old rite he thus obey'd." But what of it!?

> In Acts eleventh and sixteenth verse[29]
> This scripture truth you may rehearse.
> So let not this from bigots slip:
> That baptism only means to dip.

That the southern apostles of John Wesley were pushing hard their advance against all other groups is shown by their war song, as it appeared in one of the Mintz booklets:

> I am a soldier of the cross,
> I count all earthly things but dross:

---

29 "John indeed baptized with water: but ye shall be baptized with the Holy Ghost," was the rhymester's Biblical authority.

My soul is bound for endless rest,
I'll never leave the Methodist.

For a better church cannot be found,
Their doctrine is so pure and sound;
One reason that I'll give for this,
The Devil hates the Methodist.

They pray the most, they preach the best,
They labor most for endless rest;
I hope my Lord will them increase
And fill the world with Methodist.

The world, the Devil and Tom Pain
Have try'd their best, but all's in vain;
They can't prevail; the reason's this:
The Lord defends the Methodist.

And when that happy day shall come,
And all the Christians are brought home,
My soul will feast in endless rest
With all the shouting Methodist.

We shout so much for sinners here,
But when in heaven we do appear,
Our shouts will make the heavens ring,
When all the Methodist shall sing.

A Methodist, it is my name,
I hope to live and die the same,
I then with Jesus shall be blest
With his dear loving Methodist.

The Devil, Calvin and Voltaire
May hate the Methodist in vain;
Their doctrine shall be downward hurl'd,
The Methodist will take the world.

But when we get away from the denominational songs in Mintz we find ourselves among the hymn topics

FREEDOM IN RELIGION BEGETS FREEDOM IN SINGING.

familiar to us in the earlier Baptist atmosphere of the northeast. There are, for example, a number of new bereavement songs bewailing departed damsels.

> And is your lovely Peggy dead?

> Fair Sally's found the happy shore.

And mere males, too:

> And is dear Dennis gone?
> How short his stay has been!

The Mintz collection was one of two books[30] appearing in 1805 in which one of the most popular folk hymns of the American country tradition first appeared.[31]

> Farewell vain world I'm going home,
> My Jesus smiles and bids me come;
> Sweet angels shall convey me home,
> Away to New Jerusalem.
>
> I bless the Lord I'm born to die,
> From grief and woe my soul shall fly;
> Bright angles (sic) beckon me away
> To sing God's praise in endless day.
>
> I'll praise my maker while I've breath

---

30   The other book was Smith and Jones, *Hymns ... for the Use of Christians*, Boston.

31   Two even more widely sung texts were John Cennick's

>   Jesus my all to heaven is gone

and John Leland's

> O when shall I see Jesus
> And dwell with him above.

> And hope to praise him after death.
> I hope to praise him when I die,
> And shout salvation as I fly.
>
> And when to that bright world I rise,
> And join the anthems in the skies;
> My theme through all eternity
> Shall glory, glory, glory be.[32]

Exhortations to shun the snares of "civil mirth" are exemplified by the ditty denouncing the "dancing crew":

> O lay aside your rags of sin,
> And now consent for to come in,
> Here's clothes and all good things for you,
> Only forsake the dancing crew.

But after nine quatrains the singing exhorter sees no hope for this play-loving world:

> I must conclude and end my song,
> Young men and maidens they do throng,
> Mothers and aged fathers, too,
> Are flocking to the dancing crew.

All the text passages taken thus far from compilations between the close of the Revolution and 1806 had the strongest tang of the soil. From that time on they were somewhat less rustic. The folk-hymn stock kept growing by continuous, selective borrowing from Watts, Cennick, Newton and many unnamed writers, and by new composition. Among the happiest adoptions and/or creations of

---

[32] Mintz' *Spiritual Song Book*, p. 57. Every couplet in this hymn text became staple stock as a wandering distich in the oral folk-singing tradition. The hymn, may, indeed, represent a grouping of couplets which were *already* wandering, and not an individual composition.

this later period were:

> Brethren, we have met to worship ("Holy Manna").
>
> Come humble sinner in whose breast
> A thousand thoughts revolve. —*E. Jones*
>
> I love thee, my Savior, I love thee My Lord.
>
> Jesus, full of all compassion.
>
> Jesus, grant us all a blessing.
>
> Lift up your heads, Immanuel's friends.
>
> O how happy are they who their Savior obey.
> —*Wesley*
> Mourning souls, no longer grieve,
> Heaven is propitious. —*Thos. Hastings*
>
> My Christian friends in bonds of love.
>
> Saw ye my Savior, saw ye my Savior.
>
> What wondrous love is this, O my soul.

Special mention must be made also of three other hymns which entered the country-song tradition at that time and have remained beloved by the whole singing folk even to our day. They were Samuel Stennett's

> On Jordan's stormy banks I stand
> And cast a wishful eye.

and the two anonymous lyrics:

> Jesus, thou art the sinner's friend,
> As such I look to thee,
> Now in the bowels of thy love,
> O Lord, remember me.

and

> Farewell, vain world, I'm going home,
> My Jesus smiles and bids me come.

It seems to have been largely the Baptist sorts of singing saints who still kept the "experience" songs going. The "comes" and "come all ye's" opening such ballads run up to twenty-seven in Dupuy's Kentucky Baptist collection in 1812, and to thirty-four in *Mercer's* (Georgia Baptist) *Cluster* in 1823. The denominational rite of immersion was still strongly defended by Baptist bards:

> Go read the third of Matthew
> And read the chapter through;
> It is a guide to Christians
> To tell them what to do.
> In those days came John the Baptist
> Into the wilderness
> A-preaching of the Gospel
> Of Jesus' righteousness.
> You've read the third of Matthew;
> Go read it once again!
> You'll see none were baptized
> But did repentance bring.
> If you believe in Jesus,
> Then be immersed like him;
> As long as you neglect it
> It is to you a sin.

Those who practiced sprinkling were to take notice!

> Not at the River Jordan,
> But in the flowing stream
> Stood John, the Baptist preacher,
> When he baptized him.

> John was a Baptist preacher
> When he bapti'z'd the Lamb;
> Then Jesus was a Baptist
> And thus the Baptist(s) came.
>
> Some say that John the Baptist
> Was nothing but a Jew,
> But th' word of God informs us
> He was a Preacher too;[33]
>
> A preacher to the people,
> The Gospel truth impress'd,
> Also enforc'd their need of
> The Savior's righteousness.[34]

The old "dialogue" song style is obsolescent in this period. One new example however is

> Good morning, brother pilgrim,
> What, trav'ling to Zion?

which is "the substance of a conversation between two professors (of religion) as they meet, one going to, the other returning from camp meeting early in the morning." And Peggy Dow's collection, 1816, has a full-fledged hymnic drama with four characters—Death, Jesus, the Saint and the Narrator.

Events became portents, then as before. The Richmond theater fire of December 26, 1811, in which 70 people were killed called forth a ballad which fitted into hoary tradition. On that date ... "amusement led up her sportive train. Jollity assembled the Sons of Mirth—all was life—all was glee—when in a moment—stand in

---

[33] This quatrain has lived until today in the oral tradition of the south. *Cf. Spiritual Folk-Songs*, No. 214, for the white singers; and White's *Fisk Jubilee Songs*, p. 25, and many other collections for its persistence among black singers.

[34] Found in Dupuy's *Baptist Hymns and Spiritual Songs*, 1812, p. 50f.

trembling wonder, O my soul!—the theater of pleasure is wrapt in flames—it is converted into a house of weeping, wailing, desperation and death,—a ruinous heap, a funeral pile with this inscription: 'Be ye also ready, for in such an hour as ye think not, the Son of Man cometh.'" The song, adapted to the well known tune "Sophronia" (given in *Down-East Spirituals*, No. 206), is too long to quote in full. It opens with a scene depicting the recreation-seeking and God-forgetting Richmonders gathered in this House of Mirth when

> The shout of "fire!"—a dismal doleful cry
> Impress'd each heart with deep dismay.
> The furious blaze ascends the redd'ning sky
> Till midnight wears the face of day.
> The bells with jingling sounds and awful tolls
> Declar'd the horrors of that night.
> Alas! alas! how many precious souls
> Departed ere the morning light!
> The house of joy becomes the house of death,
> All in a moment wrapt in fire;
> The Sons of Mirth in thee resign'd their breath,
> The flames extinguish'd their desire.

Death stalked. But because some prayed "many souls were spared and plucked as firebrands from the flames."

> O may that night be never more forgot;
> Lord, still increase thy praying few.
> Were Richmond left without thy righteous lot,
> Ruin like Sodom's would ensue.

This was sung "in the Baptist Meeting-House on Wednesday, January 1st, 1812," less than a week after the disaster, "being the day set apart by the Common Hall of this city, for humiliation and prayer, in consequence of the above awful catastrophe." All this in Stark Dupuy's notable Baptist collection, the book which contained a comprehensive mass of folky hymns and thus remained popular for over thirty years and enjoyed upwards of twenty editions. It is documented that young Abraham Lincoln sang from it.

Linguistic aspects showed some improvement in these later books. But there were still contacts with the soil. Douthit's *Tennessee Zion Traveller* of 1835 tells us,

> The more gits to heaven, the lowder we'll sing,
> The more gits forgiven by Jesus my King,

—a southern example of earthy English which can be paired with the following from New Hampshire:

> O I'm so glad, O I'm so glad!
> We ha'n't got long to stay.

Dossey, 1830, found a nice big adjective:

> Jesus, thy odoriferous name,
> The heavenly choirs' transporting theme.

Past participles continued to give trouble:

> My sins hath like a mountain rose.

> For want of this the law is broke.

> My God has me of late forsook.

> For I have against him strove.

In Mintz's booklet we find:

> I feal the love of Christ my King
> A-running through my soul.

and

> When sin like a mountain
> Tremenduously great.

The River Jordan became a tempestuous sea.

> It causes me almost to tremble
> To hear how its billows do roar.
> And when to Jordan's banks we come
> And 'cross the raging billows roam.
> I'll launch my bark on Eden's (!) shore
> For Eden is my home.

The last was of course influenced by the secular chorus:

> I'll steer my bark to Erin's Isle,
> For Erin is my home.

And I must not omit the corking rhyme:

> There's no danger, my friends, if we keep persevering;
> Remember old Job's piece of money and earring.

It was chiefly during this period, say 1780 to 1830, that the great body of folk texts appeared in the country-song tradition. The whole body is listed in the first-lines indexes of *Spiritual Folk-Songs of Early America* and *Down-East Spirituals and Others*. Those indexes show the American folk-beloved hymns to mount up, after all duplicates are eliminated, to 431. This number would, however, be reduced radically if we were to exclude those which came into the folk environment merely as art riders on folk tunes; and if we took cognizance of the many song beginnings especially among the revival spirituals (to be discussed in a following chapter) which are not really "first lines" of consistent hymns but merely "wandering" lines or parts of wandering distichs or quatrains of which there were hundreds, any one of which *might* be used and scores of which *were* used as song beginnings. With this reducing process in mind our guess as to the number of consistent, organically constructed folk-hymn texts would run no higher than 200.

The Carnal Lover Is Plundered of His Tunes

> Lift up your heads, ye righteous few!
> A joyful theme belongs to you;
> Let justice seize old Adam's crew
> And all the whore's production.
> We'll take the choicest of their songs
> Which to the church of God belongs,
> And recompense them for their wrongs
> In singing their destruction.
> —Shaker *Millennial Praises*, 1813, p. 169

It takes more than a folk text to make a folk song, religious or other sorts. We have said this once before and repeat it here for emphasis. Such a text might as well remain unborn if it fails to find a tune that fits it in character and thus brings it to life. And nothing but a folk tune or one very close to the folk level will make it a folk song.

That Britain and the American colonies and then the young United States were rich in folk tunes is a fact well established by records of the times. It has been equally well established that the country folk of young America fitted, at one time or another, many scores of their religious texts to those favorite and thus far secular tunes. The only question yet unanswered is: when did this fitting trend begin?

No definite answer can be given; and this chiefly because not one of the adopted tunes was printed or otherwise recorded *with* its religious text until, apparently, long after the combinations had become orally current. There are, however, some reasonable surmises. One is that the folk tunes came into the folk-text-making-and-singing environment promptly, perhaps even with the beginning of the activity. If this surmise is correct, the earliest weddings of this sort (folk tunes with folk-made texts) took place after the middle of the eighteenth century and most of such associations were made from around 1770 through the first third of the next century.

The melodies available to post-Revolutionary American dissenters *before* they felt free enough to adopt their own genuine folk tunes were of much the same *composed* sort which, as we have seen, was propagated by the earlier Wesleyans in Britain. Some of the tunes had become popular. A few approached the folk level. One of the latter sort was "Green Fields"—widely sung with secular texts on both sides of the Atlantic long after Johann Sebastian Bach had borrowed it from German folk melodism and had started it on its way to popularity. To this tune John Newton fitted a religious parody which appeared in the *Olney Hymns* in 1779. This is the way the Newton song and its worldly counterpart began.[35]

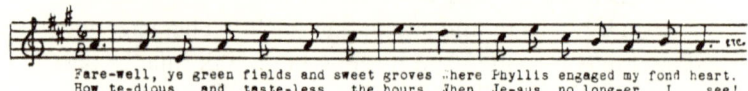

Fare-well, ye green fields and sweet groves where Phyllis engaged my fond heart.
How te-dious and taste-less the hours When Je-sus no long-er I see!

I found another song of this sort in John Glas' *Christian Songs*. Glas was leader of some groups of off-brand separatists in Scotland.[36] He provided his foot-washing-practicing and communistic groups with this hymn book but with no tunes. At the end of his book, however, Glas suggested that "many of the Scots and English song tunes answer a few of them (his texts) well." He then listed, as

---

35 See *Spiritual Folk-Songs of Early America*, No. 60. I find the secular song in America as early as 1786 in the *Select Songster*, New Haven, Conn.

36 See Benson, *op. cit.*, p. 326ff.

examples, "The Birks of Invermay," "Roslin Castle," "She Rose and Let Me In,'" "Gilderoy," "Gypsy Laddie" and a score more, and gave with each title the book numbers of those of his texts which the tunes would fit.

Just when the Glassites began to follow their leader's suggestion that they sing their hymns to popular native tunes is of course unknowable. Glas founded his eccentric sect in 1728. His *Christian Songs* appeared in 1749. I found the secular tune suggestion and list in a Providence, Rhode Island, 1787, reprint of its seventh Scottish edition. In the Rhode Island reprint we have the linking of the Glassites and their putative religious folk-singing practices with our own land. John Glas didn't come to America but his son-in-law Robert Sandeman did; and the same type of religious undertaking took root and throve for a time in New England where they were known as Sandemanians.

The song I have selected as an example of Glassite-Sandemanian song in post-Revolutionary New England follows. The tune and secular text are from the *Select Songster*, New Haven, 1786, p. 47, and the religious text is No. LXXIV in the Glassite collection.

The "Invermay" tune was Scottish and probably popular but I am convinced that it is not a folk melody. And it is worth noting that its Sandemanian singers failed to fix

SACRED HARP SINGERS AT PEABODY COLLEGE. Mose Greer, St. Joseph, Tennessee, leads a "lesson" (three songs) at the fourth convention of the Tennessee State Sacred Harp Singing Association in Nashville, first Sunday in October and the Saturday before, 1941. The youngest of the regularly scheduled early events, and the farthest north. Other conventions have met without interruption for 60 to 70 years. Photograph by courtesy of the *Nashville Tennessean*.

it in the American dissenter song tradition.

Many other examples of composed or even near-folk tunes could be cited from the singing school manuals of post-Revolutionary times. Some of them are found associated even with the folk-loved hymn texts. But the records of subsequent decades have made clear that those composed tunes remained unloved by if not completely unknown to the singing masses of country dissenters.[37]

What then did these country people of the young Republic sing? The answer came in the year 1805: they sang folk tunes. In that year a flood of light was thrown on the musical picture—light which shone backward and brightened up an otherwise folk-musically dim generation before. This flood of light was Jeremiah Ingalls' *Christian Harmony*, a veritable Comstock Lode of religious folk song, tunes and all. To understand the extraordinary significance of this book we must take a little time out to examine its musical setting and the personality of its author. First as to its setting.

All group singing at that time was religious. There was however a rather distinct cleavage within this religious group singing as determined by whether it was sung (a) in the respectable meeting house as old psalm tunes or as "Watts," (b) in the tavern sitting room as singing school music or (c) in the gatherings of the country dissident religionists as pious folk song.

For our present purposes it is unnecessary to consider the meeting-house psalm-tune phase further. It is quite pertinent however to remember that both the other movements were openly revolutionary. The singing-school movement (under way since the 1720s) represented a rebellion against what was really a religious-*musical* condition,

---

37 "Green Fields", cited above, may be looked on as an exception. "Amanda" (see *Down-East Spirituals* No. 210) is another. Both made a long-time appeal to American country singers.

that is, against the drawled-out psalm tunes. The country dissident movement, involving the Baptists, Shakers, Sandemanians, Christians *et al.*, represented a rebellion first of all against the *religious* state of affairs and only secondarily, though wholeheartedly, against entrenched church singing customs. The two movements (the singing school and the country dissident), though differing in emphasis, methods and materials, were thus in a sense parallel. Moreover, both movements throve at the same time and in the same region, the northeastern country parts.

Their differing emphasis is nowhere more evident than in their song materials. The singing schools' materials were their ubiquitous manuals of music, long-boy books of harmonized "fuguing" tunes, odes and anthems composed by the singing-school leaders themselves or "other eminent masters." The manuals of the religious rebels, on the other hand, were, as we have already pointed out, the tuneless booklets of their self-selected and homemade "hymns and spiritual songs." All the tunes they had were in their heads. As folk tunes they had been born long before and had led a time-tested life, either as secular ballad tunes or as fiddle airs, without harmonic help, notational crutches, singing masters' instruction or publishers' patronage. And this is why at least the first quarter-century of their religious use would have been a complete musical blackout for the afterworld but for the accident of Ingalls. For it was this remarkable Vermonter who, alone in his generation, borrowed the institutional singing-school song-book technic, harmonizings, book form, size and all, applied it to the country Baptist mass of folk song, published that mass of country song and thus lighted up for us the early, probably even the earliest times of religious folk singing in America.

Jeremiah Ingalls (1764–1838) was worldly enough to be an innkeeper and religious enough to be a deacon in the Congregational church in Newbury, Vermont. He was just practical and industrious enough to be a mediocre farmer and a better cooper, but musical enough to play the bass fiddle, teach singing school and lead church singing with his powerful tenor voice. And with all these occupations and diversions he seems to have been able to support his wife Mary and eleven children and compile his notable *Christian Harmony* or *Songster's Companion.*

One story about Ingalls, told by Frederic P. Wells, throws light on his genial personality.

"Returning from fishing one rainy day, he laid (*sic*) down before the fire to get dry and, impatient at the slow progress of dinner, began to sing a parody to a well-known hymn:

> How long, my people, Oh! how long
> Shall dinner hour delay?
> Fly swifter round, ye idle maids,
> And bring a dish of tea.[38]

'Why, Jerry,' said his wife, 'that's a grand tune.'
'So it is,' replied the man of song: 'I'll write it down.' And [believe it or not] dinner waited the completion of 'Northfield.'"[39]

Mary Ingalls was right. *It was* a grand tune. And Jerry gave it the "fuguing" form in which it appeared subsequently in his *Christian Harmony* and in scores of other country song collections and has been sung as a favorite of millions

---

[38] The stanza Ingalls parodied was Watts'

> How long, dear Savior, O how long
> Shall this bright hour delay?
> Fly swiftly round, ye wheels of time,
> And bring the welcome day.

[39] Frederic P. Wells. *History of Newbury, Vermont.* St. Johnsbury, Vermont, The Caledonian Company, 1902, p. 581. More about Ingalls is to be found in Frank J. Metcalf, *American Writers and Compilers of Sacred Music.* New York, 1925, pp. 121-124.

throughout the 140 years of its existence. And while long since forgotten in the region where Ingalls fiddled, fished, and fugued, it is still going strong among the legions of *Sacred Harp* singers in the southern fa-sol-la song belt. Here it is:

While the "Northfield" story shows us Jerry Ingalls the man, we must go to his book itself for an understanding of his chief contribution, which was *not* fuguing tunes.

In deciding on the basic character of his projected *Christian Harmony* he must have had his ear to the ground, that ground which had long shaken with the tread of the

Merry Dancing Baptists and their Shaker kindred. His idea was obviously to furnish those lively folk with a *tune book* of their own beloved songs. Be this as it may, he actually gathered and published no less than eighty of their favorite hymn texts and as many of the tunes to which they had presumably been sung, tunes with the tang of the upland New England turf, the tang of the British Isles song and fiddle and bagpipe tradition which the Yankees had inherited. This was Ingalls' unique contribution.

The radical nature of the *Christian Harmony* as a religious song book is well shown by the following song, Ingalls' "Separation", with which I place the organically related and subsequently recorded popular Irish reel "Johnny from Gandsey" (Guernsey) out of which he made it. The differences in detail of the two tunes may be due to their both having been recorded from memory (as "Johnny from Gandsey" acknowledgedly was), to differences between the New England and the Irish oral or instrumental tradition, or to Ingalls' own changes in the tune to make it less unsingable.

Copies of Ingalls' book are now extremely rare. Only one edition, as far as we know, ever appeared. The book was shunned, apparently, even in its own day. The rustic New England meeting-house singers at whom it was aimed didn't want any musical handbook. They could go on very well singing their tunes by memory and probably did. The singing schools had scores of better books. (Ingalls bungled badly in writing down his tunes and figuring out his harmonies.) And the urbans and would-be urbans would have none of it. This was the fate of a book which became invaluable in the history of American song, but was quite evidently born too soon. A reproduction of the *Christian Harmony* would be an extremely valuable undertaking on the part of the Vermont Folklore Society. In the meantime those interested in its songs will find forty-eight of them scattered through my *Spiritual Folk-Songs of Early America* and *Down-East Spirituals and Others*.

While religious folk song suffered in the northeast from urban frowning and competition and from an almost complete singing-school boycott, it enjoyed a happier fate elsewhere. In the country parts of Pennsylvania and all the newly settled regions southward and westward and from the time of the first settlement of these parts onward to past the middle of the nineteenth century the native folk tunes and their religious words entered into general popularity.

And this popularity was quite natural. The settlers, if they had ever been urban musically, had left their urbanity behind. Religious groups in this region were the freest of the free. The wall which had separated the churches in the older parts of the land from the singing-school institution did not exist. All the singing masters were Jerry Ingallses, purveying their musical merchandise to a friendly religious folk. Let us prove these statements by a brief survey of the tune books of this sort after Ingalls.

I have found in the period some thirty different tune books. The list begins with John Wyeth's Harrisburg, Pennsylvania, *Repository of Sacred Music* in 1810 and ends with B. F. White's Georgia *Sacred Harp* in 1844. Only six of them originated outside of the Pennsylvania-to-the-south-and-west region. All of them were hospitable, but in greatly varying degree, to folk tunes. Each book added variant recordings of the common ancestral stock. But we find single-book contributions to be modest until we reach the Leavitt, Walker and White collections, each of which embodied apparently the bulk of religious folk music of its own region; Leavitt's *Christian Lyre*, that of the northeast, and Walker's *Southern Harmony* and White's *Sacred Harp*, that of the south and west. Let us compare these three books as indexes of their times and of regional differences in attitudes toward song.

Josiah Leavitt's *Christian Lyre* appeared in two parts in the fall of 1830 and the spring of 1831. Before that summer was over he had sold 18,000 copies, and in ten years its sales had run up to 52,000 in twenty-six editions. William Walker's South Carolina book sold, according to his own figures for the period of 1835 up to the Civil War, to a total of 600,000 copies in an uncertain number of reprintings and enlargements.[40] White's big *Sacred Harp* (Georgia, 1844) enjoyed three enlarging editions and an unknown number of impressions within fifteen pre-Civil War years.

These figures alone, when contrasted to those of Ingalls' backwoods New England book of a generation earlier—one lone edition—show first and clearly a great increase in public demand for a type of song which was essentially the same in all four books. And when we

---

40 More as to Walker, his books and his interesting activities is to be found in my *White Spirituals in the Southern Uplands*, pp. 55-69 and 331-336.

consider the geography of these and the rest of the thirty-odd tune books of the period, we find weighty evidence that the love of indigenous country religious song had become much stronger and more widespread in the south and west than it ever had been in the northeastern region.

A significant difference between the one northern and the two southern song books which we are using as samples is their audience aim. Leavitt aimed at revivals and "meetings for prayer and conference," not at regular church services or at singing schools. And while both Walker's and White's title pages declared their books were for "Christian Churches of Every Denomination, Singing Schools and Private Societies," we know that their place of usefulness was less in the churches than the southeastern singing schools and singing conventions. Evidence of the difference in purpose is seen in the twenty-nine pages of the ubiquitous "Gamut, or Rudiments of Music" at the beginning of Walker's book and the twenty pages of it in White's, a feature which Leavitt had reduced to a single paragraph. Further evidence is seen in the three- and four-part harmonizings of the southern books as contrasted to the two parts only, bass and melody, in Leavitt.

Another difference between the Leavitt and the two southern books. Leavitt did very little *new* recording of "unwritten music." All but twenty-six of his folk tunes had already appeared in one collection or another; whereas Walker put into notes no less than seventy-four folk melodies from the southern and western *oral* religious tradition, that is, tunes which had not appeared, as far as I have been able to ascertain, in any other printed collection; and White was equally zealous and successful in gleaning from the same traditional sources. Walker and White along with many of their fellows were folklorists two to three generations before folklore was recognized, by that name at least, in America.

The bulk of religious songs with folk tunes appeared

in the post-Ingalls-to-White period; around 250 different examples. Add to these the Ingalls tunes and those few which had emerged before his time and the religious folk tune inventory in the middle of the 1840s contained about 350 documented examples. If variants of these tunes were counted the number would be much larger.

The larger part of these tunes has already been identified as of the old secular ballad and folk song stock. Among the 550 melodies (many of them variants of each other) in *Spiritual Folk-Songs* and *Down-East Spirituals*, I have found organic tune relationships to songs going under no less than 347 different secular titles. Samples are *Barbara Allen*, *Cruel Mother*, *Geordie*, *Little Musgrave and Lady Barnard*, *Lord Randall*, *Lord Thomas and Fair Eleanor*, *Lord Lovel*, *Rejected Lover* and *Wife of Usher's Well*.

It should be noted here that the religious folk did not confine themselves in their tune selection to any particular type of secular song. The sample titles just given happen to be of those songs now known as the "Child" ballads. But the pious songsters borrowed indiscriminately from the English, Irish, Manx, Welsh, and Scotch. They took over everything they liked whether its song text had been of love, war, homesickness, piracy, robbery, murder, or lament for the dead. They adopted even large numbers of fiddle and pipe tunes—marches, reels, jigs, and hornpipes.

But even though the American religious folk were not concerned as to the type of worldliness their favorite tunes had been steeped in, those airs had to be dyed-in-the-wool British, that is, of their own race. *All the known tunes adopted by American religious folk from sources other than British throughout the two-hundred-year period under consideration could be counted on the fingers of one hand.*

Grave and monument of barton warren stone, 1772–1844. Near the Cane Ridge meeting house where he preached lies this general in the battle of the Schismatics. He is regarded as co-founder of the Disciples of Christ.

6
Camp Meetings Are Bred in Old Kentucky. They Sire the Revival Spiritual Songs.

> O while I'm singing of his name
> My soul begins to feel the flame.
> —Southern and Western Pocket Harmonist, p. 131

The songs discussed thus far have been chiefly of two sorts, (1) hymns of praise and exhortation and (2) ballads telling of religious experience and about Biblical happenings. While these were resounding far and wide in rural America a new brand of religious folk song appeared, ushered in by a new emotional upheaval. The upheaval was the Kentucky Revival of 1800 on. The new brand of song was the "revival spiritual."

In a sense the revival in Kentucky was only a comparatively belated flare-up there of the same fires which had raged for decades intermittently in the regions east of the Appalachians. That it occurred later than the eastern revivals is explained simply by the fact that there was almost no white population in Kentucky before the last two decades of the eighteenth century when the great tide of settlement began to flow thither and then into the regions north and south of Kentucky.

That the revival fires flamed higher there is due to a number of favorable conditions. One has to do with the ethnic make-up of the population. While the eastern and northeastern settlers were largely Anglo-Saxons, the bulk of the Kentucky settlers were Gaels (Irish, Scotch-Irish, Scottish, Welsh),—people whose emotions boil at a lower temperature.

Another favorable condition was climatic-geographic. The New England backwoods pioneer farmer had to grub his few hilly acres industriously during the short summer. And during his long and comparatively idle winter nature forbade his traveling long distances or gathering in crowds greater than the little meeting houses could hold. In fertile rolling Kentucky, on the other hand, the settler enjoyed a considerable period of leisure every summer when crops were "laid by" (between the early planting and cultivating time and the later harvesting time) and when trails and roads were dry and inviting to long trips and big gatherings. And even though his meeting houses, too, were small, his comparatively rainless summers beckoned him, on gregarious occasions, out into the nearby woods or under a "brush arbor."

Still another unique condition favored the Kentucky Revival. On the eastern seaboard the religiously dissident groups had always had to fight entrenched religious and civil authority before they could have their way. They had to tear down before they could build up. In the west both religious and civil authority were at their weakest. The champions of liberty had a free hand. There, therefore, with almost no opposition, the revival could and did assume its typical non-denominational, even anti-denominational aspect. So man and nature worked together in Kentucky in making possible great gatherings in the open.

The excitement began in the summer of 1799 in the beautiful undulating lands near the Tennessee line north of Nashville, the upper reaches of the Gasper, Red, and Barren rivers. There it was that wandering preachers of different denominations, working together, attracted such crowds from such distances and for such protracted periods that they had to bring food and camping equipment. That fact alone gave birth to the institution and the term "camp meeting."

It is not necessary to go into detail as to the carryings-on at all these gatherings. The behavior patterns were not new. They differed from those emotional excesses already described as seen elsewhere and long before only in detail and perhaps in intensity. Anyone who has attended a Holy Roller meeting of present times has observed scenes of mass hysteria much the same, in quality at least, as those he can read of in the many chronicles of the Kentucky Revival. I shall retell something, however, of the great Cane Ridge camp meeting two summers later, just to show *how high* the revival fires raged.

Cane Ridge is in the Blue Grass region of Kentucky some twenty-five miles northeast of Lexington. The crowd there in the summer of 1801 was estimated at 20,000. "It was at night that the most terrible scenes were witnessed," Davenport states, following eye-witness accounts, ... "when the camp-fires blazed in a mighty circle around the vast audience of pioneers. ... As the darkness deepened, the exhortations of the preachers became more fervent and impassioned, their picturesque prophesies of doom more lurid and alarming. ... The volume of song burst all bonds of guidance and control, and broke again and again from the throats of the people while over all, at intervals, there rang out the shout of ecstasy, the sob and the groan. Men and women shouted aloud during the sermon, and shook hands all around at the close in what was termed 'the singing ecstasy.'" The "saints" and more especially those who were out to see the show would rush "from preacher to preacher, if it were whispered that it was 'more lively' at some other point, swarming enthusiastically around a brother who was laughing, leaping, shouting, swooning. ... The whole body of persons who actually fell helpless to the earth was computed ... to be three thousand. ... These were carried to a nearby meeting house and laid out on the floor. At no time was the floor less than half covered. Some lay quiet unable to move or speak. Some talked but could not move... Some, shrieking in agony, bounded about like a fish out of water. Many lay down and rolled over and over for hours at a time. Others rushed wildly over stumps and benches and then plunged, shouting 'Lost! Lost!' into the forest."[41]

I might mention here also other "physical exercises" in which those attacked by the Kentucky Revival virus specialized. I refer to the "jerks" the victims of which snapped their heads from side to side and front to back with unbelievable rapidity and vim; the "hops" where frogs were imitated; the "holy laugh," and the "barks" whose usually involuntary addicts would "tree the devil" and then get down on all fours at the foot of the tree and snap and growl.

If this wasn't perfect freedom, a chaos which had nothing in common with human behavior, it came close to it.

I have no sordid motive in re-emphasizing such scenes. Nor do I wish arrogantly to point them out as record lows from which we of so many years later have risen to such lofty civilizational heights. Our world wars and their accompanying hysteria and delusions make those Kentucky antics look very tame and innocent, civilized indeed. The point I wish to emphasize is simply that traditional polite religious behavior patterns had, in such spots and on such occasions, almost completely dissolved, become fluid in an emotional cauldron, gone over into herd behavior.

We have seen how at Cane Ridge the singing "burst

---

41 Davenport, Frederick Morgan. *Primitive Traits in Religious Revivals.* New York, 1905, p. 60ff.

all bonds of guidance," and how the crowds indulged in a "singing ecstasy" as they walked around and shook hands during their fare-thee-well "love feast." Davidson tells how, at another Kentucky revival gathering that same year (1801), no less than six different hymns were sung at one time and how "it added to the discord that they contracted the habit of singing very loud, with violent motions of the body, and in such a way as was destructive of all melody."[42] So there we have the picture. Group singing was in accord with other disorders. Its customary patterns, like other behavior patterns, had for the time being almost completely dissolved. *Almost* completely. There were still songs. Otherwise the chronicler would not have been able to count the "six" sung at once.

But what were these six? What songs did the Kentucky revivalists sing? Who furnished the songs? Unfortunately, the historians do not tell us. Davidson, the Presbyterian historian, says of Kentucky singing merely that the Methodists "succeeded in introducing (into camp meeting) their own stirring hymns." The wandering Methodist preachers were, as we have seen, beginning at that time to flout their episcopal song edicts and to take up the lively homespun songs which the self-ostracized brands of Baptists and others had been singing for many years. Bangs, Methodist historian, attributed the camp-meeting songs to John Alexander Granade "the Western Poet." His songs "perhaps became the fruitful source whence sprung the numerous ditties with which the (Methodist) Church was for some time almost deluged."[43]

No denomination has been ready to confess officially that it had fathered the definitely disreputable "ditties." From the respectable churchly viewpoint, they were either

---

42   Davidson, Robert. *History of the Presbyterian Church in the State of Kentucky.* New York, 1847, p. 131f.

43   Bangs, Nathan. *Op. cit.*, vol. ii, p. 105.

the products of individuals, the *other* denomination, or they were merely waifs. I think, however, that it is more nearly correct to conclude that the songs in question came from the memories and immediate experiences of the singing crowds,—from Baptists, Methodists, and Presbyterians of the free and less controlled turn of mind, that is, the various off-shoot Baptists, New Side Presbyterians, and O'Kellyite Methodists—New Lights all.

At first, the crowds *had* to sing from memory or sing those easy repetitive new songs which they could learn without effort, for they had no books at all. It was not long, however, before little "songsters" began to appear; and it is from these books (no tunes, unfortunately for us) made specifically for camp-meeting revivals, that we learn what those crowds sang, earlier perhaps in Kentucky, then all over the land. Many of these books were made by and for Baptists, some by and for Methodists, and many others acknowledged no author and were "for the pious of all denominations."

While the folk-hymnodic backlog (organic hymns of praise and ballads) was still glowing in the fires of the American folk religion, it was almost hidden for a time by the song tinder heaped on those fires by the camp-meeting zealots. Revival song was now completely in their hands. Individual makers of religious songs had less and less a part in the matter. Denominational authority retired disgusted from the roistering scene.

The preachers may have started a song now and then. But the real singing activity—like the real exhortational activity, the praying, the mourning, and all the "physical exercises" spoken of above—was of, for, and by the crowd. Singers controlled song. In some places and on some occasions this condition resulted, as we have seen, in perfect song anarchy. In the main, however, it seems to have been merely a record song-romping with still some method,

CANE RIDGE MEETING HOUSE NEAR LEXINGTON, KENTUCKY, built on the frontier by Presbyterians in 1791. In the summer of 1801 its floor was "never less than half covered" with prostrate, writhing casualties of the great Cane Ridge camp meeting which raged nearby. The log church was also the scene of the bloodless battle of the schismatic New Lighters against Presbyterian compulsions, a struggle which resulted in the formation of the "Christian" Church (Disciples of Christ), now one of the largest religious bodies indigenous to American soil.

new method in the singers' madness.

The results of this lyric liberty can never be fully and vividly known.

> It echoed away in the air.
> It is now gone forever.

We do, however, know something of how crowds, all crowds, tend to handle a song. We know how they "come in" on the chorus; we know indeed that crowds sing *nothing but* the chorus, or an even briefer snatch like the short-phrase refrain, or any single line or couplet of the text which strikes their fancy. We are perfectly safe in projecting this present-day folk-selective condition backward 100 to 150 years. Hence we know that we must seek the essence of the camp-meeting song contribution in those shorter or longer recurrent or repetitive passages, whatever the songs' actual overall forms and contents may have been.

The hymn books show the recurrent or repetitive process to have made modest beginnings even before the turn of the century. Even that early we find some songs the last lines of whose stanzas were either similar or identical. The unknown maker of *Come Saints and Sinners*, for example, gave every last saint and sinner a chance to come in on the last word *"union"* of every stanza as it was incanted by some exhorter-experience-singer.

> Come, saints and sinners, hear me tell
> The wonders of Immanuel
> Who snatch'd me from a burning hell
> And brought my soul with him to dwell,
> To dwell in sweetest *union*.[44]

---

44   *Cf. Down East Spirituals*, No. 9. This is the old English "tail" stanza, long and widely popular especially in fifteenth-century carols.

Also a few choruses appeared in the post-Revolutionary booklets. Each was as yet integrated with an organically constructed hymn, however, and thus kept within bounds. After every stanza of John Newton's "Stop, Poor Sinner, Stop and Think", for example, all came in on the chorus:

> O be entreated now to stop,
> For unless you warning take,
> Ere you are aware you'll drop
> Into the burning lake.

The verse-with-chorus idea spread fast in revival circles. But around the beginning of the nineteenth century, the chorus pulled loose from any and all stipulated verses or hymns. Little by little the singers got the habit of attaching the same chorus to a number of different texts. One of these wandering choruses was:

> Hallelujah to the Lamb
> Who has purchas'd our pardon!
> We will praise him again,
> When we pass over Jordan.

Still more widely sung and longer popular were the two following:

> There's glory, glory in my soul,
> It came from heav'n above;
> Which makes me praise my God so bold,
> And his dear children love.
>
> O give him glory, O give him glory,
> O give him glory, for glory is his own,
> And I will give him glory, and I will give him glory,
> Arise and give him glory, for glory is his own.

The last example above seems to represent the beginnings of the much-repetition trend. Songs of this type appeared in the early years of the camp-meeting era, as the following stanza from Mintz' *North Carolina Hymns and Spiritual Songs* of 1806 makes clear:

> O brothers will you meet me,
> O sisters will you meet me,
> O mourners will you meet me
> On Canaan's happy shore?

Then the response:

> By the grace of God I'll meet you (*thrice*)
> Where parting is no more.

This was probably sung, as were so many other songs then and subsequently, with only "brothers" in the first verse, "sisters" in the next, and so on. If this is true, we have in one song one of the earliest examples of the repetitive-cumulative and of the call-and-response technics. It is also noteworthy that, despite the absence of tunes from the Mintz booklet, there can be little doubt of this song's being an early form of the old spiritual which inspired Julia Ward Howe, nearly half a century later, in the writing of her "Battle Hymn of the Republic".

Another text-loosening factor is the one-line refrain. Its environment is usually a text made of rhyme pairs— the iambic four-accented distich which, occurring itself in twos, forms the hymn books' four-line stanza in long meter ("L. M."). The steady-going rhyme pair had long been widely used in hymns; but when these came into the livelier environment of the camp-meetings they had to be lightened up. The first stage of this lightening process seems to have been the insertion of a refrain after each pair, as for example:

> Farewell, vain world, I'm going home,
> My Savior smiles and bids me come,
> *And I don't want to stay here long.*
> Sweet angels beckon me away
> To sing God's praise in endless day,
> *And I don't want to stay here long.*

In what might be looked on as the next step in lightening up the trend, and increasing the crowd participation in song, the refrain follows each line of each rhyme pair.

> He comes, he comes, the Judge severe,
> *Roll, Jordan, roll!*
> The seventh trumpet speaks him near,
> *Roll, Jordan, roll!*

In all instances, this four-line part is followed by a chorus.

The refrain leaven thus brought the rhyme pair into the camp-meeting song life, made it at home there. In the refrain-sandwiched form, like that of "Roll Jordan", it appears in many scores of revival spiritual songs most of which are to be found in *Spiritual Folk-Songs* and *Down-East Spirituals*. It is safe to guess that the basic text was sung by one person or a few, while everybody came in on the refrain and chorus. It is easy to see how, in that sort of song atmosphere, the demand for rhyme pairs went up and the supply grew. Mass singing led to mass invention in this pattern. The pair (with or without refrains) became an independent unit. The booklets printed long series of them where the single pair functioned less as a building unit in an organic hymn poem than as a comparatively unrelated text motif. See, for example, the following text from Abner Jones' *Boston Baptist Melody of the Heart*, 1804,

p. 9.

> I'm glad I ever saw the day
> We met to sing and preach and pray.
> Here's glory, glory in my soul
> Which makes me praise my Lord so bold.
>
> Lord keep us safe while pressing through,
> And fill our souls with meekness too.
> Redeeming grace, that pleasing song,
> We'll sing as we do pass along.
>
> I hope to praise him when I die
> And shout salvation as I fly.
> Sing glory, glory through the air,
> Meet all my Father's children there.

It was the epigrammatical completeness and independence of each pair which led the singers to transplant them at will from song to song. Thus they became what have been called "wandering" rhyme pairs, homeless distichs which had a way of turning up whenever conditions were right,—that is, whenever the vocal voltage was high enough and the rhythmic gait of the song under way fitted their pattern.

So much for the text features of the revival spiritual songs. But what about their tunes?

It seems to me perfectly reasonable to assume that the revival spirituals had from the start, that is, from around 1800, the same folk tunes that we find wedded to them much later on. The fact that not a baker's dozen of the camp-meeting spiritual songs appeared *with* tunes before the late 1830s does not make it a less reasonable assumption. The ubiquitous "songsters" didn't need tunes anyway. Why waste printer's ink in publishing a tune which everybody could sing and nobody could read (in notes) or cared to? It was futile. The Ingalls experiment had proved it. And the later tune books had another reason for cold-shouldering the revival spiritual songs. It seems clear that the editors of such tunes-and-words collections as the *Christian Lyre* and *Southern Harmony*—books heavy with beautiful folk hymns of praise—excluded the camp-meeting ditties as being beneath the dignity of their volumes.

Whatever factors may have kept the songs so long from full tunes-with-words publication, the factors became in time inoperative. This type of song was to appear in full light in tune books of the late 1830s, and increasingly in those of the following decades, as we shall presently make clear.

"Crazy" Lorenzo Dow Takes Camp Meetings and Spirituals to England

> The Lord a glorious work begun
> And through America it run,
> Across the sea it flies.

In following the camp meetings' spread we may as well take the word of Lorenzo Dow who, while one of the wildest Methodist preachers of the times, was an unbelievably tireless traveler over the whole American scene and much of the British Isles; and a good chronicler, to boot.

The camp meetings spread, Dow states (in the preface of Peggy Dow's *Camp Meeting Hymns*, 2d ed., Philadelphia, 1816), first to North Carolina where one was held in Iredell County in 1802. In 1803 they were introduced into Georgia,—1804 into the Mississippi Territory, the central region of Virginia and New York State. "In the last three cantonments I attended their introduction; (I) also (attended their introduction) in Connecticut and Massachusetts in 1805." All those taking part laid aside their "party distinctions."

Leroy M. Lee, Methodist, augments our knowledge of the spread. He tells of a camp meeting at Olive Branch "in Brunswick" (County, Virginia) where the "jerks" broke out in 1806. Lee speaks somewhat disapprovingly of this "exercise" and reminded his readers that it was not the Methodists but the Baptists and Presbyterians who were to be held chiefly responsible for such excesses. It was among them, for example, according to Methodist Lee, that the dancing and the "marrying exercise" got going in Virginia. "Sometimes a whole set of them would get together and begin dancing at a most extravagant rate. Sometimes they would be exercised about getting married, and one would tell another that he or she had a particular revelation that they must be married; and if the one thus addressed did not consent he or she must expect to be damned. Thus many got married; and it was said that some old maids who had nearly gotten antiquated managed in this way to get husbands."[45]

By two years later, 1808, the camp meetings had broken into staid New Jersey. There Lee noted with disapproval a new frill. At the close of one camp meeting seven trumpeters led a procession, blowing as they went, followed by the preachers and the crowd, all singing and performing evolutions which made it possible for each to shake hands with the other, men with men and women with women.[46]

We see then that within eight years after the revival fires were kindled in the Kentucky camp-meeting environment, they had spread over the whole land. But that was not all. Mass emotional excitements are no respecters of political boundaries or even continental conformations. We know this from history. And religious revivalism is no exception. It seems to come about from conditions more general than the nationals of one land usually conceive.

---

45 Leroy M. Lee. *The Life and Times of the Reverend Jesse Lee.* Nashville, Southern Methodist Publishing House, 1860, p. 418ff.

46 *Ibid.*, p. 449.

Lorenzo Dow (1777–1834). At first "almost a Quaker" in his antagonism to all song in worship, as he admitted, crazy Dow became converted to its use when he saw its effects on camp-meeting crowds. Then the noted evangelist became zealous in propagating this sort of song—revival spirituals—all over America. He even introduced them into England.

Peggy Dow.

In the United States, it was pre- and post-Revolutionary War conditions and other growing pains which were related causally to the religious ferments of the period. In the British Isles, similar economic and political disturbances were rife at the same time—long drawn-out wars and the exceptionally cruel inroads of the machine on the handworker. In both lands, the great revivals came, it seems clear, as avenues of escape from a present world which had become unbeautiful, unsatisfying, if not quite unbearable.

The lack of restraining forces this side of the Atlantic seems to have given the frontier American revivals a start over those in Britain. At any rate, many of the typical American symptoms—physical "exercises" like jerks, dances, and barks, the uniquely American camp meeting, and the American brand of religious folk song which was part and parcel of the movement—had emerged and spread far and wide in this land before the infection of this particular epidemic of emotionalism attacked Britain. Englishmen heard about the camp meetings promptly. But hearing about them was not enough. The British revivalists had to be shown; and the man who showed them was Lorenzo Dow (1777–1834).

Dow was a Connecticut eccentric of little education and an overwrought emotional nature. As a boy, he had tried to get rid of this impossible world by the suicide route; but after his conversion by the noted Methodist, Hope Hull, he decided rather to try to make the world possible as a dwelling place.

As a Methodist preacher, Dow was a perfect failure, "too wild, too unpredictable in every way," always at odds with his organization. The early American Methodists were humble and appealed chiefly to the down-and-outers, and got them. Dow was all this and did all this; but in this, he pleased his hierarchic superiors *too* well.

While still a youth, Dow decided to leave the

American scene. He went to Ireland. There among the Roman Catholics and Methodist missioners, he was likewise cold-shouldered. In the cities, he could find no houses to preach in, was jailed for preaching in the streets, fled into the country parts where he succeeded somewhat in "stirring up the minds of the lower classes," according to the magistrates; and after eighteen months gave it up and sailed for America again.

With an "awful distress" in his mind he once more put on the Methodist harness. And sure enough, it galled him now as before; so the next four years were spent as a free-lance itinerant all over the land and notably in the south. It was during this period (1801–1805) that he saw his first camp meetings and the religious wildfire which raged there, heard his first camp-meeting spiritual singing, and became a zealot for it all.

It is necessary to remember in this connection that Dow up to this period had opposed all singing. "After my conversion," he states in his *Journal*, "I abhorred it; I felt that it abstracted from spirituality, and when (I was) in Ireland (I had become) almost Quakerized in that sentiment; but after I saw the effects of singing in the power of faith at camp meetings &c., in the awakening and conversion of sinners, I was convinced of the medium, and that singing properly was a divine employment."[47] As an apostle of camp-meeting methods, wild preaching, unhampered physical exercises, and equally free singing of the new camp-meeting folk songs, he and his wife Peggy took passage for Liverpool where they landed December 17, 1805.

In England, as formerly in Ireland, the "regular" Methodists shunned this "ape" of their ministry; but the "irregulars" of all sorts opened their arms to him.

There was a strong current of social discord flowing

---

47 Lorenzo Dow's *Journal*, Nov. 20, 1805.

through the Midlands at that time, a discord springing from the above-mentioned economic wretchedness of the working classes in that perennially "forgotten" region and aiming its hatreds at all authority, political, economic, and religious.[48] Even the Methodist Church, once the refuge of the downtrodden and outcast, had become an "authoritative and respectable institution," insistent on its own survival and intolerant of individual aberrations from its plan. It was thus chiefly from the intractables in the ranks of the Old Methodists and from the Quakers that the new English "Revivalists" came; their ranks being further swelled by other rebels and outcasts of all sorts. The name "Revivalists" was taken because they insisted on cottage prayer meetings and noisy "kitchen love feasts,"—on being emotionally dynamic.

It was into this seething current that Dow plunged and where he felt emotionally at home. And it was here, chiefly in Cheshire and Staffordshire, where, aside from occasional trips to Ireland, he "conversation-preached" (exhorted), prayed, and told about the great camp meetings in America for the next eighteen months.

"Crazy Dow" was grist to the Revivalists' mill. They had heard of him, of his American methods (his foes called them "clownish") and appearance ("more filthy than a savage Indian"); so he drew great crowds and held "melting seasons."

It was just twenty-five days after Lorenzo and his Peggy boarded ship at Liverpool again and sailed for his native land, that the first camp meeting was held in England—on Mow Cop, a point in the ridge lying between Staffordshire and Cheshire. Compared to the usual American event of this label, it must have been rather

---

48 With the practical perfection of Watt's steam engine, in 1782, the machine era began in earnest its depredations on the handworker class. The Luddite uprisings came only a little later.

tame. But there was such a crowd that they had to have four preaching stands, and "many souls were saved." Later in the same summer, they held another Mow Cop camp meeting and a still greater one at Norton-on-the-moors. These historic gatherings, though not helped by Dow's magnetic person, breathed his spirit and were run by scores of his personal friends and fellow preachers. They were the American camp meetings growing in English soil.

The stronger the camp-meeting movement grew, the more active the "respectable" denominations became in casting out the revivalist rebels, and the more these outcasts in turn felt the plain need of hanging together. Within three years, the Camp-Meeting Methodists had become a distinct community; and two years later (1812) they organized as *The Society of the Primitive Methodists* with Dow's friends and co-workers—Hugh Bourne, Peter Phillips, Dr. Paul Johnson, and others—as leading spirits.

In the records of the beginnings of the Primitive Methodists, there is, as usual in such records, little definite information about singing and song; but there is enough to make it clear that they adopted the American camp-meeting songs along with the rest of this country's revival trappings.

Dow brought along from America a camp-meeting hymn book, and some use must have been made of this book during his sojourn in the Midlands. But the first actual record touching the book is that in 1809 Hugh Bourne made much use of it in preparing *A General Collection of Hymns and Spiritual Songs for Camp-Meetings, Revivals, &c.*[49] I have not seen a copy of this 1809 edition. I have seen, however, a copy of one of the later editions. It was *A Collection of Hymns and Spiritual Songs for the Use*

---

49 See Benson, *op. cit.*, p 276. Benson gleaned from Bourne's *History of the Primitive Methodists*, reprinted in Lorenzo Dow's *Works*. See ed. New York, 1854, ii, 267.

of Primitive Methodists Generally Called Ranters.[50] Merely a glance at the first lines of the 65 hymns of this booklet (which I shall here call *Ranters*) shows them to be of the early American camp-meeting stock with only a sprinkling of new ones presumably made in England. There is a record also of how John Benton, an English itinerant disciple of Dow, "got a thousand copies of Dow's hymn-book (identical with *Ranters*?) printed" and went off missioning in the Midlands.

The English Revivalists of those early times *really sang*, and simply *because they had the New World's religious folk-made songs to sing*. It was precisely from their unrestrained singing that the Primitive Methodists got their nickname "Ranters." The story goes that the name was first applied to the group of revivalists in the town of Belper in 1814 who marched through the streets singing American spirituals as they came from their meeting house. For decades after that, the English, in indicating approval of lively and hearty group singing, said: "You sing like a Primitive."[51]

Just which of the American revival hymn books was it with which Dow infected the English? It wasn't made by Dow himself; for there is no mention in his autobiography of such activity.[52] It was therefore in all probability one of the booklets which had already begun to cater to the American camp-meeting crowds in 1805. All signs point to "Dow's hymn book" as being Smith and Jones, *Hymns Original and Selected for the use of Christians*, Boston, 1805, the best body of native revival lyrics of its time and

---

50 This book was announced as "A new Edition, Enlarged and Improved. Pocklington, printed and sold by J. Easton," n.d.

51 Walter L. Taylor, in *The Choir*, London, 1910, p. 9.

52 Peggy, his wife, made an insignificant *Collection of Camp Meeting Hymns* which appeared in Philadelphia in 1816. But that was too late; and its contents indicate that it was not the compilation which influenced the first Primitive Methodists in England.

one which was at hand right in his Massachusetts home surroundings.

All but a few songs in the English *Ranters* hymn book are to be found also in Smith and Jones. And while these songs were then, as I have said, widespread in the American tradition, there was no other book available to Dow when he left these shores for England which had them *all*.

There is also a chance that Dow carried along more than one American hymn book. He was, after all, a Methodist of a sort. And when we see the *Methodist Song* in the *Ranters* booklet:

> Come sinners, turn unto the Lord,
> And closely search his precious word,
> And when you do this truth possess,
> You may become a Methodist.

With five stanzas more—we know the song didn't come through the near-Baptists, Smith and Jones. The only other known appearance of the "Methodist Song" at that time (1805) was in the *North Carolina Spiritual Song Book* compiled by Methodist David B. Mintz. Dow may have got one of the Mintz booklets on one of his southern trips and taken it along to England; or he may have learned the ballad by heart and exported it that way. This latter guess is supported by the bad mix-up of stanzas and couplets in the English book and the leaving out of some of Mintz' militant verses.[53]

The Ranters song:

> O that poor sinners did but know
> What I for them do undergo
> Premit (*sic*) me now, my friends to tell
> What my poor frame doth often feel.

---

53 The full song as found in the Mintz booklet is given in chapter 4 of this volume.

Is a part of Dow's versified story of his own tribulations. He tells of his leaving home and friends and fighting with heat, cold, poverty, and religious persecution.

> Sometimes at night in sheds I go,
> To shelter from the driven snow;
> And there fatigued I sleepless stay,
> Smothered with smoke, or chilled till day.

The above stanza had been tidied up, probably by Hugh Bourne. Here is Dow's own version:

> But this ant't (*sic*) all I undergo
> I have to face cold winds and snow.
> I cannot sleep for want of clothes,
> Smother'd with smoke, or almost froze.[54]

The English editors, in fixing up the song so it would fit the typical tale of woe of an indigent itinerant field preacher of *their* country, deleted those lines which referred specifically to Dow's American tours:

> To Southern climes I sometimes go,
> And Northern regions to and fro;
> And to the East I go likewise,
> And in the West to win the prize.
> Across the main, to the old world,
> Where rolling billows were unfurl'd.

Bourne was not only the editor of *Ranters*. He was also the contributor of at least one significant song of his own making; the song which clinches our argument as to the American source of the English camp-meeting institution

---

54 As found in *Peggy Dow's Camp Meeting Hymns* (see footnote 8 above).

and equipment. I cite pertinent parts of Bourne's song.

> The Lord a glorious work begun,
> And thro America it run,
> Across the sea it flies;
> The work is now to us come near,
> And many are converted here,
> We see it with our eyes.
>
> The little cloud increases still,
> That first arose upon Mow Hill,
> It spreads along the plain.
> Tho' men attempt to stop its course,
> It flies in spite of all their force,
> And proves their efforts vain.
>
> Sinners at first an uproar made,
> And formalists were sore afraid,
> Because it broke their rules;
> *'Twould bring religion in disgrace,
> Begun by men so mean and base,
> And either knaves or fools.
>
> Yet still these simple souls rejoice,
> And on the hills they raise their voice,
> Salvation to proclaim;
> They preach, exhort, and sweetly sing,
> While hills and dales with praises ring,
> And sound the Saviour's name.
>
> Some of these men are meanly drest,
> Their language unrefin'd at best;
> And tho' the proud despise,
> Their labors with success are crown'd,
> The pow'r of God does still confound
> The wisdom of the wise.
>
> They preach and pray with all their might,
> Sinners constrain'd do cry outright,

> But, when by grace restor'd,
> Those who were weeping, sore distrest,
> Soon as they find their souls are blest,
> Rise up and praise the Lord.
>
> Christians at camp-meetings unite,
> And free from bigotry and spite,
> Both sects and parties fall;
> There's no respect of persons shown,
> But all as one their Saviour own,
> And Christ is all in all.

New editions of the American camp-meeting spirituals, as compiled in the *Ranters* book, appeared in the 1820s. But the sixty-five original hymns were not then enough to satisfy the needs of a sect that was growing up. So they cut the long ones in two and, instead of dipping deeper into the richly flowing American well-spring of folk-made spirituals, the Primitive Methodists enlarged their hymn book by job-lot additions made largely by Bourne and William Sanders.

When, about the middle of the century, their conference ordered the use of a nice new book made respectable by the elimination of hymns of the *Ranters* sort, large sections of the connection rebelled. The "Old Hymn-Bookers" sang from the Bourne books as long as copies were to be had.

There is much evidence that American camp-meeting spirituals—the Dow introductions and others of later date—were widely sung in English, Scottish, Irish, Manx, and Welsh revival circles throughout the years of the greatest popularity of the same songs in America, that is, up to around 1870.[55]

---

[55] The evidence has been collected in part by Anne G. Gilchrist. See *JFSS*, viii, pp. 61-95.

Farmer William Miller Dates the World's End

> In eighteen hundred and thirty-one
> A glorious jubilee begun.
> —Baptist, *New Conference Hymn Book*,
>   1837, p. 24.

> In eighteen hundred forty-three
> Will be the Year of Jubilee
> —*Hymns of the Second Advent Band*,
>   1843, title page.

Mass religious hysteria or super-emotional revival comes in waves. History makes this clear. Crowd excitement flares up, spreads by contagion or imitation to the most susceptible, spends itself, dies down. The masses remain quiescent for a time; then another outbreak. The American colonies and the young United States experienced three broad movements of this type; the Great Awakening, the Kentucky Revival, and the great Millennial Excitement now to claim our attention.

In all revivals hellfire had been the chief threat. "Turn, sinner, turn while there is yet time!" Judgment Day *might* come at *any* time! Then your chances of salvation would be suddenly reduced to naught! This was, to be sure, a *real* threat, but it was after all only a remote possibility. The old world didn't seem to be tottering; this despite all tokens and the camp-meeting folk's insistence that the very outpourings of the Spirit at their revivals showed the world's end to be just around the corner. So all Last Day threats gradually lost their punch.

The 1830s however were to see a brand new wrinkle in the world's fate idea; a shock treatment for chronically careless souls which was to stir up the entire land to an emotional excitement pitch as high or higher than that of the Kentucky Revival of a generation before and was to reverberate literally around the civilized world for the next hundred years; an idea born in the brain of a Vermont farmer, William Miller.

Others had been talking about the Day of Wrath. Miller *did* something about it. He picked up his Bible and his pencil and reckoned. The result: The end of the world would come in the spring of 1843. After demonstrating his calculations rather widely before church congregations he got a Baptist license to preach and became, from 1831 on, a pulpit power.

To Baptists, Congregationalists, Methodists, Christians, Shakers as well as to run-of-mine sinners Miller's new idea was electrical. They flocked to him. His meetings quickly took on all the camp meeting aspects, with shouting, falling-out, rolling—the whole list of hysteria symptoms.

Nature seemed to work hand in hand with Miller. Biblically promised portents appeared in plenty during the years of waiting. Cholera scourged the nations in 1832; the "stars fell" in the meteoric shower of 1833; rings appeared around the sun and "crosses" were seen in the sky. Every comet was a sign. Halley's arched the heavens in 1835, and the Great Comet of 1843 was perfectly timed.

But the Judgment Day, though thus effectively harbingered and dated to a day by Miller and his even more imaginative followers, failed to appear. Miller went over his figures and found a slight error due to different calendars. The fateful Last Day was put off until October 22, 1844.

Miller had made no attempt at first to establish a separate denomination. He worked with all sects. But when the initial friendliness of other groups turned to opposition he stepped down from borrowed pulpits, bought a big tent and went over the country on his own. (That was at the time of the date revision, 1843.) In this independent venture he was powerfully helped by Joshua Vaughan Himes, scantily educated, one-time boy-exhorter, and long the pastor of the First Christian Church in Boston. To the "Moses" Miller, Himes with his funds and fiery zeal became an "Aaron." The far-reaching tent tours and unbelievably great quantities of printed propaganda (periodicals, tracts, hymn books, tune books, etc.) carried their alarming Messianic message to the millions.[56]

The intensity of the stir may be better understood if we cite from contemporary documents. *The New York Herald* of January 16, 1843, brought a report from Boston that "the Miller excitement is at once tremendous and awful." *The Louisville Courier* told how, during a Millerite protracted meeting in the spring of 1844, "the excitement

---

56 In 1843 Miller took his message beyond New England, to New York, Philadelphia, Cleveland and northern Ohio, Cincinnati (very successful), Western New York State, Buffalo, St. Louis (mobbed), Great Lakes region, Indiana, Louisville (Himes preaching), St. Louis again (successful), Missouri, Illinois to the western frontier largely with the Methodists, Iowa and Wisconsin. Penetration of the south by the leaders was delayed by their reputed anti-slavery views and reports of their stirring up the blacks in the north. Miller had been mobbed and jailed even in New Hampshire for his emancipation talk. In the fall of 1844 however public opinion in the south relented (found he was not intent on freeing the slaves on these trips) and Miller was permitted in Delaware, Virginia and Maryland. Both blacks and whites became greatly excited in Kentucky, Tennessee (where it had "rained blood") and Mississippi. The above information is derived from the unpublished University of Wisconsin doctor's dissertation made in 1930 by Everett N. Dick, entitled *William Miller and the Adventist Crisis, 1831–1844*.

was ... greater than one ... could imagine." Rich and poor, white and "niggers" jammed Miller's great tent. There was much "praying, singing, shouting, groaning and weeping bitterly." Among blacks "hundreds ... (were) crying and making the most hideous noises."

Even the advertisers in the press made use of the uproar: "THE TIME HAS COME when consumption can be classed with the curable diseases—Wistar's Balsam of Wild Cherry." The press led the mob ridicule of the excitement with cartoons and the like, thus helping to heighten the tumult. The Millennials came back at the fun makers with the scriptural, "There shall come in the last days scoffers."

"Miller madness" filled many a suicide's grave and put many more in the insane asylums. The "religious insane" admitted to the Worcester, Massachusetts, asylum grew from four to twelve per cent of all admissions during the years 1841–1843. The years 1843 and 1844 were, according to Everett N. Dick, "among the greatest revival years in the history of the United States." "Full half the inhabitants (of Albany, New York) were crazy with religious excitement," the correspondent of the *New York Herald* wrote to his paper early in 1843.[57]

The furore grew as the end of the "Tarrying Time" (October 22, 1844) approached. Believers even closed their shops, resigned their positions, left their crops. One faithful saint donned his ascension robes, climbed a tree and jumped to his death. Dick calls attention to an eyewitness' story of the Rochester, New York, Millennialists on the "last day" appearing in the *New York Morning Express* for October 28, six days later. The eyewitness states that on the 22d all was bright and fair at Rochester. Adventists were up early and met in prayer. All was ready. One last convert was taken to the nearby river to be immersed.

---

57 Dick. *op. cit.*, p. 204.

VERMONT FARMER STIRRED AMERICA. WILLIAM MILLER, 1782–1849, reckoned out the time of the end of the world, kept millions of credulous ones stirred up for a decade. His miscalculation did not keep the Millerites from growing into the strong Seventh-Day Adventist denomination.

Those remaining in the meeting house sang:

> Now is the hour of Time's farewell,
> And soon with Jesus we shall dwell,
> The speeding moments hasten on
> And they soon all will be gone.

With the chorus:

> We're going, we're going,
> We're on our journey home.
> We're traveling to a city just in sight.[58]

But nothing happened. "Still the cold world! No deliverance!" cried Elder Luther Boutelle, expressing the "Great Disappointment" of all the Millennialists. From the outside came torrents of we-told-you-so ridicule. Gloom settled on all the faithful. The "shut door" doctrine (the Bridegroom had gone in and shut the door) obtained among some. Jesus *had* come. Only the "timists" saw new portents and set new dates for the coming. The rank and file, however, of the then organized Second Adventists gradually got away from all dating and began giving thought to other religious matters like immersion, Bible authority, sanctification, seventh-day Sabbath and the abstinence from coffee, tea, tobacco, and flesh foods—some of which special interests persisted among the varieties of Adventists which eventually appeared, and contributed perhaps more to the permanent traits of the Seventh-Day Adventists as we know that world-embracing denomination today, than did the original Millerite "millennial madness."

The Millennial furore must not be interpreted as affecting only those who eventually came under the Second (Seventh-Day) Adventist banner. We have already seen

---

58 *Idem.*, p. 250.

how Miller worked at times with organized denominations. Nearly half the traveling Millerite propagandists in the 1840s were Methodists. A fourth of their number were Baptists. Congregationalists, Christians and Presbyterians had a goodly share in the propagation; and even Dutch Reformed, Episcopalians, Quakers and Lutherans took a hand. Thirty Methodist ministers in Maine proclaimed the End according to Miller. The idea obsessed the Baptists almost completely in some sections, as in Vermont. In the early years of the Furious Forties the adherents to the already great Baptist and Methodist connections increased 50 per cent, first in the north and east, a little later in the south. We shall have a word to say presently as to how the excitement touched also the newly organized Mormons and fed the mounting fires of the Shakers. We might state here also, just for completeness of the record, that there was some causal relationship between the millennial furore of the times and the mania of other religious or near-religious groups which flourished then; for example, that of the Teetotalers and of the anti-war, anti-slavery, anti-Masonic and anti-Catholic groups.

Camp meeting scene. From a drawing by Rider. His conception was sympathetic and lent a dignity that was probably rarely observed at such gatherings. Note that men and women are seated separately. The costumes indicate a date in the 1840s.

Songs of the Second Coming

> Are your lamps trimmed and burning?
> Are your vessels filled with oil?

The Millennial messengers marched on with music. They found a great stock of end-of-time songs which had been developed by the revival excitement of a generation before. These fitted the new idea, or were revamped to fit it and put to work. Not only the specific judgment-day songs were taken over; the whole body of camp-meeting spiritual folk songs was recalled for service in the new revival ranks.

The Millerites' chief book of song was the *Millennial Harp* which Joshua Himes hurried through the printer's hands in the fall of the supposedly fateful 1843 in the faith that it would be on sale before all earthly transactions were over. Most of the book's 213 songs express a longing for the Last Day or an exhortation to be ready for it; or they paint word pictures of its terrors for those whose lamps are not "trimmed and burning."

A typical end-of-time song in the *Millennial Harp* is *You'd Better Come to Jesus*. You'd better be a-praying, you'd better get religion, you need a hope of mercy, come try a bleeding Savior—in this, our day. You'll see the Judge descending, hear the trumpet sounding, see the dead arising, hear the thunders roaring, see the world a-burning, hear the sinners crying, hear the saints a-shouting. The saints will shine in glory in that great day.—Each of the foregoing phrases is the germ of a repetitive stanza.

Similar is *The Last Trumpet* with its chorus:

> For Gabriel's going to blow by and by, by and by,
> For Gabriel's going to blow by and by.

So get your hearts in order. You will see the graves a-bursting. You will see this world on fire. There will be an awful shaking. How will you stand it, sinner? You will wish you were forgiven. But saints will not be frightened. They'll rise and meet their Jesus. He will lead them to his kingdom. Then the warfare will be ended. We will shout above the fire, at the end of time.

They changed the chorus of the then old-time *I Belong to This Band* song to:

> I will be in this band, hallelujah!
> In the Second Advent band, hallelujah!

Other veteran songs called back to the colors during the limited period left to fight sin were: *Don't You See My Jesus Coming, The Last Lovely Morning, Day of Judgment, Hark, the Waking Up of Nations, Will You Go, Bound for the Land of Canaan, I'll Try to Prove Faithful, O There Will Be Mourning, O Turn Ye*.

Despite the Great Cataclysm's first failure to arrive they sang on:

> Bless the Lord, we need not fear,
> For Daniel says he'll come this year.
> Both prophets and apostles, too,
> Their writings show this doctrine true.
> Then, waiting brethren, let us sing,
> He will not tarry long.

In wishful imagination:

> Now we feel the Advent Glory
> While the Savior seems to tarry,[59]
> We will comfort one another
> And be trusting in his name.
> Are your lamps all burning?
> Are your vessels filled with oil?

Miller died five years later, 1849, but this song echoed on. Naturally the singers had to change its tense:

> We *have felt* the Advent Glory
> While the vision *seemed* to tarry,
> When we *comforted* each other *etc.*[60]

And five years after Miller's demise the "timers" still felt confident enough to sing:

> O praise the Lord, we do not fear
> To tell the world he'll come next year.
> In eighteen hundred fifty-four
> The saints will shout their suff'rings o'er.

One of the most infectious and lasting of the Millerite songs was *The Old Church Yard*. In it one feels the measured tread of the hope-filled masses marching to the graveyards where:

> Ye shall see your Lord a-coming

and shall

---

[59] The "tarrying" season proper began with March 22, 1844 and ended October 22 of the same year.

[60] From *Pilgrims' Songster*, Concord, New Hampshire, 1853. *The italics are mine.*

> Hear, the band of music, (*thrice*)
> Which is sounding through the air.

He'll awake all the nations. There'll be a mighty wailing. O sinner, you will tremble. Ye will see the saints arising. Angels will bear both the dead and the living, all arrayed in spotless white, before the Savior. Then we'll shout our suff'rings over.

The tune was what carried *The Old Church Yard* far and long. During its early years it appeared in the concert repertory of the famous Hutchinson Family. Under the title *The Old Granite State*, the tune with a text telling of the Hutchinsons' New Hampshire home and introducing all members of their family, present and absent, became a sort of theme song for their program and was carried by the noted ballad singers widely in this land and even across the Atlantic. The burnt-cork minstrels parodied the Hutchinson text and sang the same tune to a song they called the *Old Virginny State*. It was also in the time of the tune's popularity that the Teetotalers took it up.

> The teetotalers are coming, (*thrice*)
> With the cold water pledge.
> *Chorus*
> We're a band of freemen, (*thrice*)
> And we'll sound it through the land.

The above samples may serve to characterize the millennialists' contribution to religious and secular folk song during the general revival activities of the late 1830s and the 1840s. From the evidence the time must be looked on also as one during which the revival spiritual songs took their last great spurt,—were perhaps more widely sung than at any other time since the first emergence and vogue of that romping sort of song forty years or so before.

10 Shakers, Mormons Ride the Millennial Wave

> Now do we find great increase
> While shaking spreads from west to east.

The Shakers (United Society of Believers in Christ's Second Appearing) were never a large sect; but they were always colorful. Like other radically separatistic religious groups they got their start through one strong individual. Emotionally high-strung Ann Lee with a few followers had fled British economic oppression and the persecution which was visited on Shaking Quakerism and had come to America. During the Revolutionary War this little party of refugees established a colony in the upper Hudson River valley. But even in the land then freeing itself from the "tyrant's galling yoke" they were persecuted, jailed for pacifism and treason. And they throve on it, naturally.

Their early growth up to around 1800 was, as we have already seen, due largely to accessions from the wrought-up Whitefieldian New Lighters and from offshoot Baptists who were well suited emotionally to the Shaker type of life. By that time they had grown to eleven colonies (settlements), all in New England and the eastern margin of New York State.

When they heard of the uproar in Kentucky they rightly sized it up as a disturbance which would produce

Shaker material. The three missionaries they sent into the west found no trouble in canalizing large numbers of those frontier people who had been stirred to religious frenzy by the great southern and western revival—and in establishing one after another seven settlements in Kentucky and southern Ohio.

The disciples of Mother Ann had sung from the start. But possessing no body of song suited to their own purposes, they borrowed at first largely from the ubiquitous sober psalm-tune stock, the songs which the later Shakers still used to some extent and called "solemn songs." Paul Petrovich Svinin tells how he heard the Shaker colony in Alfred, Maine, between 1811 and 1813, singing "the Psalms of David ... in an abominable drawl."[61]

It was in the western branch of Shakerism that a great new wave of song arose. The wave was at first organic with that of the Kentucky Revival as a whole. The Shakers quickly altered the texts or made new ones to suit their "Mother Ann" (Ann Lee) worship, and in this guise the song swell swept eastward into the older settlements.

The new songs out of the west were of two general sorts, Shaker-historical ballads and "exercise" songs, the latter so-called because they accompanied their dancing and other "exercises."

Richard McNemar—Gael, Presbyterian, then Schismatic and Shaker, strong-lunged preacher, singer, writer of hymns, in Kentucky and Ohio—was a powerful propagandist of Shaker song. It was he in all probability who wrote also the historical ballad from which I take the following stanzas:

> At Manchester, in England, this blessed fire began,

---

[61] Avraham Yarmolinsky, *Picturesque United States of America*, New York, Williamn Edwin Rudge, 1930, summarized the travel notes of Svinin, Russian traveler-diplimat-artist. See Yarmolinksy, p. 22.

And like a flame in stubble, from house to house it ran.
A few at first receiv'd it and did their lusts forsake;
But soon their inward power brought on a mighty shake.

The rulers cried, "Delusion! Who can these Shakers be?
Are these the wild fanatics, bewitchèd by Ann Lee?
We'll stop this noise and shaking, it never shall prevail!
We'll seize the grand deceiver and thrust her into jail!"

Before their learnèd council, though oft she was arraign'd,
Her life was uncondemnèd, her character unstain'd.
And by her painful travel (travail), her suff'rings and her toil,
A little Church was formèd on the European soil.

This little band of union in apostolic life
Remain'd a while in England among the sons of strife,
Till the Columbian Eagle, borne by an eastern breeze,
Conveyed this little kingdom across the rolling seas.

Hail, thou victorious gospel and that auspicious day
When Mother safely landed in Hudson's lovely bay!
Near Albany they settled and waited for a while,
Until a mighty shaking made all the desert smile.

About four years she labour'd with the attentive throng,
Confirm'd the young believers and help'd their souls along.
At length she clos'd her labour and vanish'd out of sight
And left the Church increasing in the pure gospel light.

How much they are deceivèd who think that Mother's dead!
She lives among her offspring who just begin to spread.
And in her outward order there's one supplies her room,
And still the name of Mother is like a sweet perfume.

> Since Mother sent the gospel and spread it in the west,
> How many sons and daughters are nourish'd from her breast!
> How many more conceivèd and trav'ling (travailing) in the birth,
> Who yet shall reign with Mother like princes on the earth![62]

Later McNemar wrote also "An Allegorical Detail of the Entrance of Mother Ann's Gospel in the West, in the Year 1805."[63] Its burden was somewhat as follows: The good ship New-Light was launched in 1801. Elijah was her captain and John was boatswain. They sailed away from "this vain world of sin," but were soon opposed by a man-of-war which halted them because they were not "elected from all eternity." The warship's captain was "bold Calvin" (Calvinism as espoused especially by Presbyterians). The New-Light steered away and met another enemy ship, the Arminius (doctrine of free grace, named after the Dutchman, Jacob Harmensen). They escaped again. "Four years we plowed the ocean when met by the Royal Ann which had come forth to meet the New-Light and bring her safe to land." The New-Light's boatswain hailed: "To what empire do you belong and what is your captain's name? Let us know where you go, whence you came." "Our captain," somebody on the Royal Ann answered, "is Emanuel; to Canaan we pertain."

The good ship New-Light steered "Leeward." A difference of opinion arose on board (referring to denominational

---

62 From *Millennial Praises*, Hancock, Massachusetts, 1813, p. 79ff.

63 I found it in *A Selection of Hymns and Poems for Believers*, by Philo Harmoniae (McNemar's pen name), Watervliet, Ohio, 1833, p. 136. The facts behind this allegory are to be found in MacLean, J. P., *The Shakers of Ohio*, Columbus, Ohio, 1907, p. 252ff.

break-ups in Kentucky?). Crew insulted officers. Some deserted the ship in a "longboat." A few remained. The longboat approached the Royal Ann. After the justifiably mutinous crew had been summoned to throw overboard "every sin," their longboat was taken in tow

> Till we enter'd Salem's harbour
> And found the land of peace.

The upsurge of "exercise" songs among the western Shakers and their subsequent flooding of the eastern communities is made perfectly clear by Edward Deming Andrews.[64] He has also analysed the Shakers' first hymn book, the *Millennial Praises* (1813) mentioned above, and, with the assistance of the present author, has pointed out numbers of clear instances of influence from the song fires of the interdenominational and non-denominational early camp meeting environment.

The Shakers grew steadily during the first three decades of the nineteenth century and reached their all-time high in membership during the 1840s, that is, during the Millerite Millennial years. There must have been discouraging times, however. The following Shaker song "Newyear 1833" indicates as much:

> Come let us all be of good cheer!
> We've liv'd to see another year—
> We have been carried safely through
> The tedious year of 'thirty-two.
> Whatever may have cross'd our path,
> There's nothing yet that's shook our faith.
> But from the early date of 'five (1805)
> That precious faith is kept alive.[65]

---

64 *The Gift to be Simple. Songs, Dances and Rituals of the American Shakers.* New York, J. J. Augustin, 1940. See especially pages 9-16.

65 Philo Harmoniae (McNemar), *op. cit.*, p. 53.

The Miller excitement fed generously into their hopper. Thousands of victims of that hysteria joined the Shaker ranks both before and after the Great Disappointment.

These later crowds of Shaker neophytes did not, however, bring in their Millennial songs wholesale from the outside as did the throngs of thirty to forty years before. The sect of their refuge was already well provided with End-of-the-World songs and was, moreover, confirmed in its own song-making ways. The few songs which did go over to the Shakers at this later time were naturally of the lively revival spiritual sort. I point specifically to the following songs, reproduced by Andrews, as showing outside influence: "Come Life, Shaker Life",[66] "Love, Love, Love",[67] "Followers of the Lamb",[68] "Lay Me Low",[69] "When Cheer Fills",[70] "Mother Lucy's Birthday Song",[71] and "Brave Soldier".[72]

A comparison of the two following song texts will show rather strikingly that the Massachusetts Shakers and the Rhode Island Baptists were birds of much the same feather even though they may not have flocked together.

---

66 Tune reminders of "Heaven Born Soldiers," and "Weeping Mary," *Spiritual Folk-Songs*, Nos. 195 and 164 respectively.

67 See German folk song "Hop, Hop, Hop"—tune resemblance noted by Andrews.

68 See "My Bible Leads to Glory", *Spiritual Folk-Songs*, No. 233. The song was widely sung in the 1840s.

69 For melodic similarities see *Spiritual Folk-Songs*, No. 100, and *Down-East Spirituals*, No. 64.

70 See *Spiritual Folk-Songs*, No. 155.

71 See *Down-East Spirituals*, No. 158.

72 See *Spiritual Folk-Songs*, No. 178.

From the Shaker *Millennial Praises*, Hancock, (Mass.) 1813, p. 239.

> When the Lord in ancient days
> Set Mount Sinai in a blaze,
> O the trumpet's awful sound!
> How it shook the solid ground!
>
> When the burning flames appear'd,
> Guilty rebels shook and fear'd;
> Now we see a hotter blaze
> Kindled in these latter days.
>
> Now the flame begins to run,
> Now the shaking is begun;
> He that gave creation birth
> Shakes the heavens and the earth.
>
> Though the wicked stand and mock,
> They shall not escape the shock;
> All the world will have to say,
> Shaking is no foolish play.
>
> Shaking here and shaking there,
> People shaking everywhere;
> Since I have my sins confess'd
> I can shake among the rest.
>
> We'll be shaken to and fro
> Till we let old Adam go;
> When our souls are born again,
> We unshaken shall remain.
>
> Some will boldly try to stand,
> But the Lord will shake the land;
> Sinners who shall dare rebel
> Will be shaken into hell.

From the Baptist *New Conference Hymn Book*, Pawtucket, Rhode Island, 1837, Second part, *Original Hymns*, p. 20.

> The Lord that sits upon the throne,
> Will shake the earth and shake it soon,
> He'll shake all nations far and near,
> And fill the world with awful fear.
>
> He'll shake the land, he'll shake the sea,
> He'll shake the mountains where they be,
> He'll shake the rocks both high and low
> He'll shake the rivers that do flow.
>
> He'll shake the kingdoms of the earth,
> He'll shake the proud in awful wrath,
> He'll shake the kings upon their throne,
> O what a shaking time will come!
>
> He'll shake old Babylon the great,
> That tramples on the church and state;
> Her tow'ring walls though built around,
> He'll shake, and shake, and shake them down.
>
> He'll shake the devil down to hell,
> And chain him there in the dark cell;
> Destroy his subjects in his wrath,
> And shake his kingdom from the earth.
>
> He'll shake the church that's on the sand,
> He has declar'd she shall not stand;
> He'll shake false prophets from the world,
> And they shall down to hell be hurl'd.
>
> He'll shake false preachers that do preach
> He'll shake the doctrines that they teach;
> And they must have their just reward
> Who have despisèd Christ their Lord.

The Mormons, too, were millennialists. Their proper name "The Church of Jesus Christ of Latter Day Saints" showed it. "Latter" to them meant "almost the last." From their backwoods start in 1830 they grew rather quickly, within the millennial excitement period and in some measure because of it, to the stature of a denomination which ramified widely in America and abroad. The revivals of their early years were marked by most of the emotional "exercises" which marked those of other ecstatic sects. From their start also they laid great stress on group singing.

The earliest Mormon hymn book, compiled by Emma Smith, wife of Joseph Smith, founder of the sect, consisted largely of the quieter traditional American country lyrics.[73] But later editions of this book and new collections show clearly that the initial inclination of the Mormons to sing the religious folk songs of other frontier denominations soon disappeared and they began making their own songs in a much more urban style.

A trace of the earliest leaning toward indigenous songs may be seen in the later hymn books in the hymn "Come, Come Ye Saints" which was to be sung to the tune of "All is Well." And that they were not inhospitable to currently popular secular and religious tunes, even though composed by non-Mormons is shown by their "O My Father", sung to Stephen Foster's "Gentle Annie" tune and to McGrannahan's "My Redeemer"; and by "O Ye Mountains High", in which the Mormons sang of their new-found home in Utah to H. S. Thompson's popular tune "Lily Dale". Of the lively revival spirituals I have been able to find but one trace, and that in a song book for Mormon children. It was the chorus:

---

73 *A Collection of Hymns for the Church of the Latter Day Saints.* Kirtland, Ohio, 1835.

> O I can't stay away, O I can't stay away,
> I love my little meetings so, I can't stay away.[74]

The above mentioned songs are rare exceptions. The great body of early Mormon song, both tunes and words, was and remained individually and learnedly made by and for Mormons.

---

74 See *Spiritual Folk-Songs*, No. 153.

11 Revival Spiritual Tunes Come Into the Open at Last

> Shout, children, shout you're free!
> Christ has bought your liberty!

The millennial excitement did one good deed for those of us who would trace America's religious folk-singing ways. It was during and after that furore and in the song books which reflected it that the recording of the tradition was completed. The more sedate part of the tradition, that of the *folk hymns of praise* and the *religious ballads* had long since come out into clear light. We have seen this and spoken of it above. The livelier *revival spirituals*, however, had appeared only in part. We had the words in many "songsters," but the tunes-with-words recordings of the revival spirituals had been extremely few. We have suggested reasons for this such as the reluctance of music publishers to descend to the camp-meeting song level and the general feeling that everybody knew the tunes and that it would therefore be pointless to publish them. But whatever the objections, they were waived progressively during the 1840s to 1860s, the decades which gave us at long last the full words-with-tunes aspects of the tradition which, as we are sure, had been very much alive for at least a long generation before that period began.[75]

The first to bring a considerable grist of "whole" revival spirituals was the 1842 Boston booklet, *Revival Hymns*.[76] In the same town, same year, appeared *Revival Melodies or Songs of Zion*,[77] with revival spiritual songs borrowed from *Revival Hymns*. A third Boston book with this sort of tunes, the *Millennial Harp Designed for Meetings on the Second Coming of Christ*, appearing a year later, 1843, was discussed in Chapter IX. It contained twenty-three revival spirituals fourteen of which were new tune recordings. A fourth northeastern book of this sort appeared two years later, Baptist revivalist Elder Jacob Knapp's *Evangelical Harp*, Utica, New York, 1845. Its 14 revival spirituals (along with 33 folk hymns and their tunes) are largely the same pieces as those found in the other three books just mentioned.

Neale, in the Preface to *Revival Hymns*, affirms our findings as to the brand newness of his musical undertakings. Certain songs, he states, "though ... familiar in prayer and inquiry (revival) meetings, have now (and in this book) for the first time been published." One such tune is undoubtedly on his page 39, 'I want to Wear the Crown', a rousing spiritual. Its vigorous line, "My dungeon shook, my chains fell off," he felt necessary to explain in a note as "figurative language." And as to the line "He spake and made me laugh and cry," he assures his less emotional readers that not everyone "must expect to have just this exercise."[78] Things were already getting civilized,

---

75 See above, page 82.

76 *Revival Hymns...* Selected by the Rev. R. H. Neale, set to some of the most familiar and useful *Revival Tunes* by H. W. Day, A.M., editor of the (Boston) *Musical Visitor*. Boston, 1842.

77 Copyrighted 1842. I have examined the "seventeenth edition" still bearing the same date. No editor is given.

78 The song is reproduced in *Down-East Spirituals* as No. 295.

up Boston way.

That it was an act of audacity to publish these unrefined native American revival spirituals in Boston, right under the nose of Lowell Mason and the other Better Music Boys, was clearly recognized by the compilers. Joshua Himes, in his Preface to *Millennial Hymns*, meets his expected disapprovers ahead of time with: "Some of our hymns, which might be objected to by the more grave and intellectual, and to which we ourselves have never felt any great partiality, have been the means of reaching, for good, the hearts of those who would not otherwise have been affected." And thus he justifies their presence in his book.

Neale brings witness to the considerable age which the revival-spiritual tradition had reached by 1842. His note on

> Shout, shout, we're gaining ground,
> Halle, hallelujah!
> Satan's kingdom is tumbling down,
> Glory hallelujah![79]

reads: "This hymn and the original melody, which have been so useful in revival seasons *for more than half a century* (italics mine), and which, it is believed, have never before been published together, were lately procured after considerable search, from the diary of an ancient servant of Christ, bearing the date of 1810." We should note also that the servant of Christ is unnamed. Such contributors of real folk-songs still had their inhibitions. Neale got many old songs, he states in his Preface, from "private Christians and sweet singers in Israel, whose modesty forbids the mention of their names." More's the pity.

It should be noted that in publishing these revival

---

79 The song is reproduced in *Down-East Spirituals* as No. 240.

spirituals, tunes with words, the *down-east Yankees beat the southern compilers "to it" by two years*.

Despite their somewhat later start, the southern country song book makers were soon to catch up with their northeastern colleagues and to enter into a sort of contest among themselves to see who would be able to collect and publish the most revival spirituals the soonest. In the southeast *the Sacred Harp, A Collection of Psalm and Hymn Tunes* ... by B(enjamin) F(ranklin) White and E. J. King, Hamilton, Harris County, Georgia, 1844, was the first and chief torch bearer of the revival spiritual songs. It presented 25 examples of this type, mostly newly recorded from the Georgia oral tradition. Six years later (1850) White added 22 more spirituals; and in the Supplements of 1859, 1869, 1911 and 1936 they were increased by 12, 20, 8 and 1 respectively.

An attempt by William (Singin' Billy) Walker to outdo his brother-in-law B. F. White in purveying the popular revival spirituals to the southern country singers came one year later. Walker, the reader will remember, had ten years before published his *Southern Harmony*, loaded with beautiful folk hymns of praise and religious ballads but without a single revival spiritual. He called his new 1845 book the *Southern and Western Pocket Harmonist, intended as an Appendix to the Southern Harmony; Embracing the Principal Hymns, Songs, Choruses and Revival Tunes Usually Sung at Protracted and Camp Meetings of Different Denominations of Christians Throughout the Southern and Western States*. Its nineteen (only) songs of the sort under consideration proved but weak competition with White's offerings; and he failed to make up for his general revival-spiritual shortcomings in later enlargings of his *Southern Harmony*.

By far the biggest single-book and single-edition batch of revival spirituals produced in the South was in

John Gordon McCurry's *Social Harp* of 1855. There were 64 of them, 37 appearing there for the first time anywhere.

McCurry and White were both Georgians. Their books were compiled from the Georgia and South Carolina oral tradition, one which lived and throve chiefly among the country Baptists and Methodists and in the essentially non-sectarian fa-sol-la singing conventions of the 1850s. The tradition, as embodied in the *Sacred Harp*, has persisted there and thus to the present day. Our debt to those two compilers is great. Without their work we should know very few of the revival spirituals of the southeastern tradition as it lived during the twenty years preceding the Civil War.

There were, to be sure, some flaws in the revival spiritual recordings by McCurry, White, Walker and others. None of the compilers was quite equal to his musical task. All three strove to fit the revival material into the singing-convention molds by writing a continuous part for each of the three voices (treble, tenor and bass), thus wiping out all signs of the original give-and-take between leading singer and chorus.

The three-part harmony itself, while old in the singing-school and singing-convention tradition, was quite foreign, or at best incidental, to the revival singing atmosphere. It not only obscured the relationship between leading singer and group, it blurred also the melody, the essential element in the revival songs. But though it is hard to distinguish the melody, when listening to fa-sol-la singing, one can easily find it on the printed page. It is always the "tenor." And the text aspects tell us almost unfailingly what was once sung by the leader alone and what by the whole group as refrain and chorus. So, while the alterations of the songs are regrettable, they by no means nullify the great contributions to our knowledge of revival songs made by McCurry in his *Social Harp*, White in his *Sacred Harp*, and Walker in his *Southern and Western Pocket Harmonist*.[80]

At the close of the Civil War the northeastern oral religious folk-song tradition was brought into even clearer relief by Joseph Hillman of Troy, New York, in his *Revivalist*, apparently the first notable book to devote its pages to religious folk song in that region after the Boston booklets of which we have spoken. It contained 469 hymns and only a few less tunes; and it was so widely used in its region that edition followed edition and its size grew eventually to 592 items. Among these I have counted 21 religious ballads, 93 hymns of praise and *99 revival spirituals*, all of the folk type. These 99 included most of the songs which had appeared in the Boston books 25 years before during the millennial excitement and they were very largely the same songs which had been recorded in the meantime in the southeastern books, though they differed from the latter in text and tune detail.

When I first examined the *Revivalist* I suspected influence from the south. It was in view of the text and tune differences just mentioned, however, that I soon saw my suspicion was unfounded. And in all my searchings I failed also to find a single source reference (among the many) or other evidence pointing to the south. I think therefore that we must look on Joseph Hillman as the William Walker or the Benjamin Franklin White or the John Gordon McCurry of the northeast,—as the recorder of the oral folk-singing tradition of his region just as the other three had been the inscribers of essentially the same folk custom in theirs. The composite labors of the four have been of untold value.

But to return to the revival spirituals themselves for a

---

80 The stories of these books, their authors, singers and singing institutions are told in *White Spirituals in the Southern Uplands*, Chapters VI to XI.

Conservator of Down-East Spirituals, Joseph Hillman (1839–1890) of Troy, New York. His collection, *The Revivalist* (150,000 copies), recorded the entire body of religious folk song in the largely oral tradition of the northeast as carried on in the mid-nineteenth century chiefly by Methodists. Photograph of an oil painting.

little summary. After having been sung all over the land for nearly half a century, as evinced by their *texts* in scores of camp-meetings "songsters" throughout the first 30 to 40 years of the nineteenth century, the "whole" spirituals, tunes as well as texts, came out of hiding. The millennial furore, arising in the northeast, gave that region the start in presenting them. The southeast followed quickly and published them in great quantities, practically the entire southern store appearing within the 25 years following 1844. And just before those 25 years were over the northern oral tradition was equally completely presented in *one* book, the *Revivalist*.

Here we must be reminded, however, that in all the country books discussed the folk hymns of praise were presented in far larger batches and in far greater total numbers than were the revival spirituals. All of the books discussed contained also some examples of the smaller folk variety, the religious ballads.

Old-Time Religion Outmoded. Social Gospel Comes In.

We have now traced the early religious folk-singing practice and its tardy book emergence. The evidence has justified us, I believe, in looking on the period from 1780 to 1830 or perhaps later as the time of the tradition's birth, youth and greatest vigor. This was also the period, we have seen, when the folk participated most widely in, and enjoyed most undisputed control—for better or worse—over its own private and institutional religious affairs. All the evidence has pointed moreover toward the interdependence during these decades of that mass-controlled religion and mass-controlled song. If this view is correct, then it would seem perfectly obvious that the weakening and failure of the one would bring with it the palsying of the other. It was just such a weakening which soon set in and which we shall now discuss.

The *practical weakness* and *ideal strength* of the Old-Time Religion was its individualism, its anti-institutionalism or "no partyism." That was, as we know, the pervading spirit of those Revolutionary times. "The best governed people is the least governed." This sounded fine. It was supposed to work in political affairs. Why shouldn't it work in religious affairs, too? It should. But it didn't.

Americans were still gregarious humans—still members of Western European civilized society. Very soon even the perfect-freedom-seeking masses began to realize this. They began to ask themselves whether perhaps religious institutions were bad as such, or whether they, the mass minions of freedom, could not perhaps make new institutions in religion (as in government) that would be "good" ones,—institutions which would reject all the "bad" phases of the old sects. After all, they, the dissenters, were very much alike. Why couldn't they march together under new banners? This sort of reasoning must have preceded the first steps in denominational re-integration, the remodeling of the old sects and the building from the ground up of the many-named new Churches which have appeared in the United States in the past century and a half.

The most notable early example of sectarian re-integration is offered by the "Christian Church." The chroniclers of this sect show it to have originated by the merging of three groups, one in New England recruited from the centrifugal Baptists and led by Elias Smith and Abner Jones, one in Virginia and North Carolina consisting of the schismatic Republican Methodists led by James O'Kelly, and the third (and perhaps the most important group) in Kentucky composed of similarly unruly offshoot Presbyterians led by Barton Warren Stone. In a remarkably short time after these leaders had broken away from their older denominations, that is by 1804, the three independent groups (Stoneites, Smith-and-Jonesites and O'Kellyites) discovered that they believed in and practiced precisely the same thing, that is, that Christ and the Bible should be their sole guide, so they did the natural thing,—joined forces and formed a loose group that was 100 per cent American folk-religious. At first they all felt the self-imposed no-party injunction. They obeyed this, they felt sure, by calling themselves merely Christians.

Others might call them what they would.

> Nor do we scorn the New-Lights' name
> Christians are all New-Lights,—Amen!

It was Elias Smith himself, I suspect, who composed the following new and illuminating verses to the older popular "Union" ballad:[81]

> More than ten years have rolled away
> Since I did testify and say,
> Aside all party names I'd lay
> And make the name of Christ my stay,
>   And join in Christian Union.
>
> As at the time I did not know
> One on this earthly ball below
> That thus with me would join and go.
> I ask'd some brethren. They said, no,
>   We cannot join such Union.
>
> My name is dear, said brother P. (Presbyterian)
> And so is mine, said brother C. (Congregationalist)
> Then loud spake out my brother B. (Baptist)
> My name's the dearest of the three,
>   Away with such a Union!
>
> Then brothers F. and M. did say (Free-Will Baptist, Methodist)
> Our heart is join'd with you this day;
> The name is nothing, yet we may
> Not throw our names out of the way,
>   But still we'll join in Union.

The "Christians'" founder thus did find a few that now were of his mind—who searched the Scriptures for to find

---

81 Given in full in *Spiritual Folk-Songs of Early America*. No. 37.

A NEIGHBORHOOD SACRED HARP SINGING at Liberty Church, Lawrence County, Tennessee, December 7, 1941. George Pullen Jackson leads a "lesson." Photograph by Ed Clark for *Life Magazine*, used with their permission.

OLD-TIME RELIGION OUTMODED

> The good old way, and leave behind
> All things that hurt this Union.

His twelve-stanza appeal closes with

> Brethren of every name, to thee
> Who do inquire if good there be
> In Christian Conference, come and see,
> In Christ there is true liberty,
>   Enjoying Christian Union.

Thus no-partyism went over painlessly to what Lorenzo Dow called "all-partism."

The Christian Church became, as it happened, one of the strongest of the regroupings which came directly out of the camp-meeting cauldron. Other groups gathered or driven forward directly or indirectly by that same revival excitement and sticking in some instances to their old party names, with perhaps a qualifying word joined, were the multiplying brands of Arminian (free grace) Baptists, the Cumberland Presbyterians, Disciples and Shakers. All of them specialized on one phase or another of the new-found freedom in creed, behavior and group control. Each of them, like the Christian Church, embodied for a time and in varying degrees what we have called the individualistic folk religion or, as it is now referred to, the Old-Time Religion.

During the first half of the nineteenth century, pioneering times proper, the Old-Time Religion in these various patterns had a fairly favorable cultural environment. It throve and was not forced to make radical adjustments. With the second half of the century however and with the Civil War out of the way a new time, a new cultural outlook and a new religious trend appeared. (I say new, though its beginnings had of course been long before.) The Old-Time Religion was slowly but surely getting out of style. The old-time revival, camp-meeting style, in which all had an equally uproarious part gave way slowly to soberer occasions, to solemnly persuading Moodys assisted by sweet-singing Sankeys. The frontier influence became less pervasive. Cities were growing and making the country countryfied and crude. All this meant that religious institutions were faced with the alternatives of adaptation or eventual extinction. Most of them chose adaptation.

It is beyond the bounds of our present task, as it is beyond the competence of the author, to portray in detail the religious aspects of the past two generations. All that is needed here is to stress the facts, well known to historically minded churchmen, (a) that the Old-Time Religion of 100 to 150 years ago and Modern American Protestantism are quite different entities, and (b) that the former is all but dead while the latter is very much alive, institutionally at least.

The Old-Time Religion was, as we have seen, a personal and highly emotional affair wholly between the individual and his God. Modern Protestantism (still called "Protestantism" with less and less reason, since it protests against practically nothing), in giving up the personal-emotional Gospel has taken on in its stead the social-ethical-esthetic Gospel. It is vital to remember this. To gain any clear understanding of American religious trends we must not forget that a typical Baptist of 150 to 200 years ago was entirely different from the average member of the First Baptist Church on Main Street today. We must recognize also the same radical difference between the old-time American "shouting" Methodist who struggled against such sinful things as pews, bells, steeples and "civil mirth," and the modern Methodist in his imposing American Gothic social center; between the

Millerite on the hilltop dressed in white and ready for the sweet chariot, and today's Adventist whose churches are in every civilized land; between the ecstatic deluded and persecuted follower of country-boy Joe Smith and a typical member of the present urban, world-covering Church of Jesus Christ of Latter-Day Saints; between the New Side, Cumberland and other rampant Presbyterians of long ago and the conservative folk who now walk reunited under that denominational banner; and finally, between the old deeply emotional and widely persecuted Quakers and the highly respectable and universally respected modern Society of Friends.

The radical difference between the moderns and their denominational forerunners is no less striking than the similarity today of their offspring groups—Social Gospel churches one and all; a similarity which, increasingly recognized, is leading to widespread movements for unification.

To look upon the Old-Time Religion as now *completely* dead is, however, a Mark Twain exaggeration. But it is very weak. Its last stand against modern religious urbanity has been made in forgotten places—mill towns, mountain coves, city slums. In such places among the Holiness folk, Pentecostals, the Church of the Living God, the much persecuted Jehovah's Witnesses, Primitive Baptists and their likes, its fire still glows in different colors but with much of the old heat.[82] Some of the old spirit is left also in remote segments of otherwise citified denominations, like the "Christians" in parts of West Virginia and

---

[82] Thomas Hart Benton thinks of these ecstatic sects and their doings as perhaps "...the last decadent flare of that Protestantism which accompanied the rise of capitalism over the world. Maybe its lunatic, disintegrating wildness is a portent, a symbol of the end of social ways which are also disintegrating, wild and irresponsible."—*An Artist in America,* New York, McBride, 1937, p. 109.

Pennsylvania. Southern blacks, where they are *still* unurbanized, are still largely old-time religious.

Two further examples of those who have stuck to the old, for better or worse, are the German Baptists and the Shakers. The German Baptists, or Mennonites, though splitting up rather often among themselves, have persisted uniquely in their religious (and cultural) folkways, those of seventeenth and eighteenth century pietistic Germany. Finding themselves thus out of step with the modern capitalistic-competitive culture they had no part or heart in making, they are now striving, as a group, to leave it and to find a home in South America, far (as they hope) from war compulsions and other stresses of a modernity which they despise and from the land where they feel they can no longer live and act "according to the dictates of their own conscience."

The Shakers have become victims of their own unchanging principles in a changing world. Their practice of communism might have been less lethal but for the fact that it was bound up with the death-bearing principle of celibacy. Their institutional blood had to be renewed by extramural transfusion. And as American society developed, it became harder and harder, finally impossible to keep their ranks filled. The great intake due to the pre-Civil War millennial excitement was the last real Shaker accession. When that generation of neophytes grew old and began dying off, the end of the company of Mother Ann's Children was in sight. Today their vast properties are being or have been sold off; and only a few score of oldsters are still awaiting death.

Old-time Songs Are Pushed Aside

> The most belov'd on earth
> Not long survives today;
> So music past is obsolete,
> And yet 'twas sweet, 'twas passing sweet,
> But now 'tis gone away.[83]

Religious folk songs have survived chiefly in those few places where the Old-Time Religion has endured among the older changeless groups, and in about the same measure. Elsewhere they, too, are on their way to oblivion.

The most typical religious intransigents in America today (aside from the Mennonites, not considered here because they did not take up our American country song tradition) are the Primitive Baptists of many varieties. And they stick best to the old folk songs. Only in the last few decades has their hoary "unwritten" song tradition been made available to them in notated form. Their little congregations in remote parts of the southern uplands and lowlands—meeting usually once a month—have their choice of using either the *Primitive Baptist Hymn and Tune Book*[84] or *Good Old Songs*[85]. Both of these comprise selections from the tradition as the compilers found it in Benjamin

---

83 From *Church Harmony*, Chambersburg, Pennsylvania, 1841, p. 300.

84 Compiled by John R. Daily, Madisonville, Kentucky, 1902.

85 Compiled by C. H. Cayce, Martin, Tennessee, 1913. Now published in Thornton, Ark.

Lloyd's *Primitive Hymns* (700 of them, no tunes)[86] and in fa-sol-la four-shape tune books such as the *Southern Harmony, Sacred Harp, Hesperian Harp* and *Olive Leaf*. The singers pay little attention, however, to the compilers' tunetext combinations. The hymn words are the thing. When the elder announces the number of the hymn to be sung, "suits the tune" and "hists" it, the singer will find the words in the book where announced, but the tune, while always an old folk melody, is often in another part of the book and associated with an entirely different hymn. The Old School (also called Primitive) Baptists, extremely changeless predestinarian groups in New Jersey towns (Hopewell is one) use a *Hymn and Tune Book* which is similar to the manuals used in the south, but has some intrusions from the standard hymnody of other denominations.[87]

The city Baptists too (the Primitives call them "Missionary Baptists"), in the south at least, have still some sparks of the old religious fire in their souls and a few drops of the old-song blood in their veins. In the *American Hymnal*,[88] widely used in their southern urban churches, I find a dozen or so songs of the old stock, songs such as "How Tedious and Tasteless the Hours", "Come ye Sinners", "Amazing Grace", "How Firm a Foundation", "Holy Manna", "I Will Arise" and "Old-Time' Religion". Some of them are ruined by the editorial majorizing of their old modal tunes. But the cluster is still significant. The northern Baptists have, as far as I have observed, freed themselves completely from their one-time country-song tradition.

The Seventh-Day Adventists stand alone among the

---

86 First appeared in Greenville, Alabama, 1858. Latest printing, La Mesa, California, 1935.

87 It was compiled by Silas H. Durand and P. G. Lester of Southampton, Bucks County, Pennsylvania, 1886.

88 Compiled by Robert H. Coleman, Dallas, Texas, c. 1933.

South Union, Kentucky, Deserted Shaker Colony. "Center House" (*top left*) built in 1824 in the midst of four thousand acres of Shaker-owned land. Deserted in 1921 when the colony was sold and closed out.

Hotel (*bottom left*) at South Union railroad station. Shaker-built in 1869.

Last living member of the colony, Mrs. Alice Wintuska Bass (*above*), 94 years old in 1940, "could outdance all the young folks" even in her eighties. Still sings Shaker dance songs to the merriment of her great grandchildren. Shaker name for South Union was "The Holy Fountain of the Lord Jehovah." Photographs by the author.

well organized and wide-spreading denominations who have held true to the old-time songs they were brought up on a hundred years ago. There seems to have been little weakening of their loyalty to the old home stock from the time of the Boston *Millennial Harp* (1843) up to the present. Their *Hymn and Tune Book* of 1886, still in wide use, contains no less than 53 of the old songs. The immensely popular 'Old Churchyard' of William Miller's end-of-the-world days is still there; but its text has been dressed up. Some "improving" editor made over the militant chorus:

> Hear the band of music (*thrice*)
> Which is sounding through the air.

into

> While the choir of angels (*thrice*)
> Shall be chanting through the sky.

A remarkably unyielding survival of the old-time songs in actual singing practice is observable today in the *Sacred Harp* circles in the south; a practice which, as we have seen, stemmed a hundred years ago chiefly from the "unwritten music" of different folk sects. These singers, themselves largely Primitive or "Hardshell" Baptists, meeting in regularly dated conventions throughout the year but more frequently in the warmer months, keep alive not only the whole body of Old Baptist folk hymns of praise; they revel also in the revival spiritual songs which, as we have seen,[89] appeared increasingly on the pages of the *Sacred Harp* from its first edition in 1844 onward. (This revival-spiritual type of song, we should state, is not heard in white Primitive Baptist church services today. They prefer the soberer folk hymns of praise.)

---

89 *Cf.* above, page 121.

The *Harp* singers enjoy immensely still another type of *folky* if not *folk* song. It is the "fuguing" song which they took over from the eighteenth-century northeastern singing-school tradition after it wandered southward when the United States was still young. A sample is Jeremiah Ingalls' "Northfield" on page 71 above. The *Sacred Harp* has for a hundred years welcomed everything folky but has consistently refused the use of its pages to all else whether it be the art hymns of a Haendel or a Lowell Mason or the popular gospel hymns and their even more popular offspring, the gospel songs.

There are some religious environs where we might expect to find the old folk songs, but do not find them. The Methodists—a fine example of adaptive denomination—had the practical sense once upon a time, while fighting off the religious folk songs officially and excluding them from their *authorized* collections, to allow their revivalists—from Mintz and Lorenzo Dow onward—to use them freely in swelling the ranks of Methodism. But that was once-upon-a-time. The "vulgar" songs have long since served their purpose and been cast off. Modern Methodists use the standardized stock of urban congregational song.

"Vulgar" things, however, have a way of becoming in time "antiques." It was in the mood of the hunter of antiques that editor George B. McCutchan of the Methodists' most recent hymnal re-examined "the hymns of the ages," found "many of surprising merit" and introduced them into his book.[90] We must assume that this note in the hymnal's preface refers in part to early American religious folk songs, for we find in this excellent collection no less than fourteen examples drawn from the old native stock.[91]

---

90 *The Methodist Hymnal.* Edited by Robert G. McCutchan. Nashville, Dallas, Richmond, Publishing House of the Methodist Episcopal Church South, 1935.

91 The songs are, 'Green Fields', No. 349; 'Amazing Grace', No. 209;

The Presbyterians, direct line, never sang the religious folk songs. This denomination was always too well behaved and reserved. While the American revivalists were developing a native folk lyricism 150 years ago, these conservative carriers of Calvinism were still debating whether they should stick to the psalm tunes ("Metrical monstrosities," the poet Addison called them) or become dangerously modern by singing Watts. Thus they never got the indigenous songs in their denominational bloodstream.

The Mormons' exposure to the infectious lyrics was too slight. They quickly outgrew them, as we have seen above, and have now a hymnody which is on a par with that of the most dignified denominations.

A number of sects of the "country" sort—the Nazarenes, Pentecostals and Church of God (Holy Rollers) for example—grew up during the gospel hymn epidemic and caught the ailment. Still others, like the Disciples of Christ and the Church of Christ, though older and with a remote good-old-songs background have been too loosely organized denominationally to withstand the temptations of temporary song styles. In the cities they have therefore gone over long since to Lowell Mason and his school and, in the country, to the gospel songs.

That the Shaker songs—close to the folk from the start—will vanish as a living tradition with the last Shaker is self-evident. I feel for this reason all the more fortunate in having been able to record two Shaker songs, one from the singing of Mrs. Alice Wintuska Bass, the last living member (in 1940) of the once large and prosperous

---

'Beloved', No. 346; 'Nettleton', No. 23; 'Parting Hand', No. 229, tune somewhat altered, different text; 'Friends of Freedom'. No. 281; 'Plenary', No. 521; 'Romish Lady', No. 436, tune only; 'How Firm a Foundation', No. 315(2); 'Lenox', No. 211; 'Candler', No. 311; 'Avon', No. 373; 'Meirionyad', No. 454, a version of 'Burk'; and 'Campmeeting', No. 303, related to Asa Hull's 'Hark, Listen to the Trumpeters', see Tune Comparative List here, No. 79.

Shaker community at South Union, Kentucky (almost on the spot of the first camp meeting in history).[92] The other was sung by Will Barnett, an elderly black man, who in his youth had been employed in the same colony.[93]

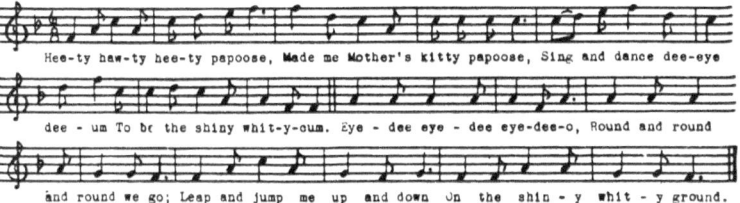

Hee-ty haw-ty hee-ty papoose, Made me Mother's kitty papoose, Sing and dance dee-eye dee - um To be the shiny whit-y-oum. Eye - dee eye - dee eye-dee-o, Round and round and round we go; Leap and jump me up and down On the shin - y whit - y ground.

The above song illustrates the long followed bent of the Shakers for singing dancing songs with nonsense texts and calling them "Indian" and what not. Mrs. Bass learned this when she was but a little girl in the South Union colony. She left with the last eight oldsters when they moved from the community in 1921.

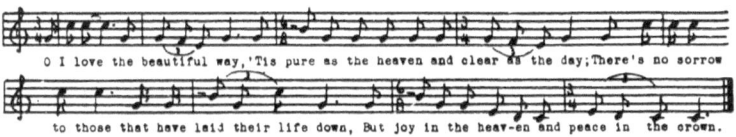

O I love the beautiful way, 'Tis pure as the heaven and clear as the day; There's no sorrow to those that have laid their life down, But joy in the heav-en and peace in the crown.

---

92 Sung by Mrs. Alice Wintuska Bass, Shaker, age 94, Auburn, Kentucky, September 8, 1940.

93 Sung by Will Barnett, age 68, at South Union, Kentucky. September 8, 1940. He had learned it of the Shakers, Will Bates and Elder Logan John, who sang it there about 1894 as a good-by song when Elder Joseph Holden was leaving the colony for New York.

APPENDIX

PAGES FROM *THE EASY INSTRUCTOR* (1802). Title page (*top*) and score for "Schenectady" from page 41 (*bottom*).

Buckwheat Notes

In the matter of its popular acceptance and actual use, the graphic symbolism of music has remained far behind that of speech. That is to say, inability to read music is far greater than language illiteracy. Among the many reasons for this acknowledged condition, one is without doubt the comparative complexity of notated music—with its variety of note-values, rests, clefs, staffs, keys, rhythmic intricacies, etc., etc., as it confronts the would-be learner. It is the purpose of the author to tell in this article of a little-known but far-reaching and successful rural American attempt at simplifying the problems of reading music, especially for the beginner in singing.

The English-speaking people who, in the seventeenth century, streamed into the eastern coastal parts of what were to become the United States were, as it seems, wholly unable to read music notation. "Music" with them meant merely singing, that is congregational church-singing, by rote. And even that lean phase of music had sunk, after a few generations of settlement and pioneering, to an unbelievably low level. The tunes available to those sitting in the "meeting houses" had shriveled to a paltry few, and those few were miserably sung. Indeed, congregational singing must have been—if we may believe reports of the times—like some devil-take-the-hindmost responsive reading of the present day.

In New England, where conditions in the early days were not much better, people bestirred themselves in the

The Alabama State Sacred Harp (Four-Shape) Singing Association in Birmingham, Alabama, July 1929.

first part of the eighteenth century. John Tufts and Thomas Walter produced two little song-books which stressed the importance of singing "by note," increased the visible supply of tunes, made a brave attempt at showing what part-singing was, and led singing into its first temptation to escape the control of the church, if not of religion, and to pursue an independent career in singing-schools.

In this singing-school movement—about the only strong domestic one in music for over one hundred subsequent years—appeared the first real need of musical notation. For notes, Tufts used the letters F, S, L, and M, placed on and between the conventional five staff-lines. These were the initials of the four syllables, fa, sol, la, and mi, which will be recognized perhaps as the notes of that system of solmization which the colonists had brought with them from England, and had not yet totally forgotten. Their ascending scale was sung fa, sol, la, fa, sol, la, mi, fa, and not do, re, mi, etc., the diatonic sequence which, though now familiar to us, was a much later importation. Walter's book had the regular notes with diamond-shaped heads which were then customary in church-tune books. But he used the fa-sol-la-mi series of note names in his explanations of the rudiments of music, just as did all subsequent singing-school teachers and all American books of such songs for over a hundred years afterward.

In the singing-school the rustic musical neophyte had to join with others of the same voice-range in singing their part over and over "by note" before being allowed to use the words. And in this practice the difficulty in learning that a note in a certain staff position was fa in one tune and la in another of a different key was very real. It was a hindrance to reading which the earnest teacher would fain have removed. But the way to surmount this obstacle did not appear until about the year 1800, when two teachers, William Little and William Smith (of whose lives almost nothing is known), produced a song collection called *The Easy Instructor, or, a New Method of Teaching Sacred Harmony*. Its second edition (the only one of which I have seen a copy) was printed at Albany, N. Y., in 1802. In this book each of the four notes was provided with a different shape-head. Fa was ◣, sol ◻, la ◢, and the rarely used mi was ◆. The ascending scale therefore appeared as follows:

This was a boon to the singing-school scholar. For it dispensed with all the formerly necessary guessing as to the name of a note, once that name was associated in his memory with a particular shape; and this association of shape with name helped the singer to identify the melodic or harmonic character of the notes.

There has been some doubt expressed as to whether Little and Smith were the real inventors of these note shapes. That doubt has been caused by the fact that Andrew Law, an active singing-school teacher in Connecticut, got out a book a little later which he called a "Music Primer," in which the same shapes were used but without staff-lines to support them, the notes being merely raised or lowered, much as they would have appeared with lines. Law claimed the system as his own. His claim may have been technically correct. He may have intended to appropriate merely the sequence (ascending) of the note shapes (which was ◻fa, ◻sol, ◻la, etc., as opposed to Little and Smith's ◣fa, ◻sol, ◢la, etc.), and the discarding of the staff may have been his idea. But the five lines, as Law soon discovered, could not be done away with. The sequence of note shapes offered by Little and Smith was preferred to that of the Connecticut teacher and came into general use by country singing-schools.

When we say "country" singing-schools we mean very nearly all of them. For, as fast as cities developed, just so fast did music and musical practices in those centers tend to conform to the more advanced ones of Europe. And to just that extent did the domestic singing-schools find it more agreeable to take their homespun religious music and its notational "helps to read" into the culturally virgin stretches of the West and the South.

An indication of the popularity of the new notation may be found in the number of books in which it was used. I have found thirty-six different books of this type which were published during the fifty-seven years following 1798. And there are doubtless many more. Nineteen of the thirty-six known books apparently were used chiefly in the South, the other seventeen in the North.

Timothy B. Mason's experience in Cincinnati, in 1834, may serve to illustrate the popularity of "patent" notes there and the forces which worked for and against them. It seems that Mason came to these musical backwoods with the self-imposed mission of converting them to urban ways. He prepared an excellent song-book, *The Ohio Sacred Harp*, and intended to drop it as a round-note bomb into the shape-note camp. But "such was the ignorance of any other kind of notes [than the shaped ones] west of the Alleghenies, that when the Messrs. Mason [Timothy and Lowell, his brother] published their . . . book . . . they were obliged, against their convictions of right, to suffer the publisher to make use of such notes to accommodate the wants of that region."[1]

After selling fifty thousand shape-note copies of the *Ohio Sacred Harp*, Mason carried out his fell purpose of a round-note edition. Urban competition was stronger, better organized and "higher class." So the Yankee singing-school master took his national scheme to the smaller places where round notes and organs did not corrupt the singers of harmonic parts and where concertizing "families" did not break in and monopolize the tunes.

Rural singing-schools and their inevitable shape-notation had a happier fate in the South. For there the unfavorable factors, urbanity, itinerant providers of concert music, church organs, and the like, were completely absent. The inland and highland South was filled by those who debarked at Philadelphia and Baltimore. They were Scotch, Irish, Welsh, and German, people who fell right in with the Yankee singing-school masters who were already working in eastern Pennsylvania and thereabouts, and strengthened the singing element among the great masses of settlers who wandered southwestward and westward. In this broad section, the upland South, no musical notation other than the shape sort was known for decades. Of the nineteen singing-books "for churches, singing-schools and private societies" compiled in this section between 1815 and 1855 the most widely used were *Kentucky Harmony* (Harrisonburg, Va.), *Columbian Harmony* (Wilson County, Tenn.), *Missouri Harmony* (St. Louis, Mo.), *Genuine Church Music* (Winchester, Va.), *Southern Harmony* (Spartanburg, S. C.), *Union Harmony* (Maryville, Tenn.), *Sacred Harp* (Hamilton, Ga.), *Hesperian Harp* (Wadley, Ga.), and *Social Harp* (Andersonville, Ga.). Each compiler was a teacher and propagandist of shape-note singing. Naturally, he boosted his own song-book, usually

---

[1] N. D. Gould, *The History of Sacred Music in America*, Boston, 1853, p. 55.

over as wide a territory as possible, in numberless singing-schools, and—beginning around 1850—also in singing conventions. The earlier books were printed from type in various little home-town print-shops. The later ones were made from stereotyped plates, usually in Cincinnati or Philadelphia.

The fa-sol-la solmization and its four-shape notation, though immensely popular for half a century, were doomed from the moment when the do-re-mi habit took root on these shores. In the 1840s the South, apparently the last stronghold of the ancestral solmization practices, began to feel the presence of the new notes. And the Civil War period marked the end of growth.for the four-shapers' notation and its books. But, although not a single new compilation came out after that period in four-shape notation, at least two of the older books remained in wide use. One of these, William Walker's *Southern Harmony*, after a popularity extending over more than fifty years following its appearance, is today all but extinct, with "singings" being held annually in but one place, Benton, Ky. The other, "*The Sacred Harp* of 1844," is still fully alive, with many singing-schools conducted in New England's best manner of one hundred and fifty years ago, and with hundreds of weekly, monthly, or yearly singings or conventions in the territory which extends in a broad belt from northern South Carolina westward, taking in practically all the hill country as far as Oklahoma and northeastern Texas, leaving out the flat coastal lands farther to the south, and Tennessee, and the territory north of it. The "Fasola Folk," those who still apply the Elizabethan names to the notes of songs made in pre-Revolutionary America and sing them with the help of the 132-year-old "patent notes," still number from about 30,000 to 50,000 souls.

One may take it reasonably for granted, therefore, that the complete disappearance of that lusty vestige of our early culture remains far off.

But the story of the Fasola four-shapers and their rural guilds is not the whole story of shape-notes. Nor is it the bigger part of that story, quantitatively. When the do-re-mi style reached the domain of the rural southern songsters, it split them into two factions, those intransigents mentioned above who preferred to "seek the old paths and walk therein," and the less conservative and eventually far larger group which saw the advantages of "seven names for seven notes." But even these "moderns" were loath to give up the tried and trusted "glorious patent notes of William Little and William Smith." While the shape-noters were in this quandary, Jesse Aikin, an enterprising Pennsylvania singing-school teacher and songbook compiler, came forward with a voluminous do-re-mi book called *The Christian Minstrel* (Philadelphia, 1846); it was printed in a notation in which the four old shapes were preserved and three others were added, making the ascending diatonic scale appear as follows:

The popularity of the Aikin innovation is proved by the fact that his book enjoyed one hundred and seventy-one editions and by the even more eloquent fact that he very soon had many imitators. These imitators were made to feel that the shapes, at least the three new ones, were Aikin's own property. So they used the old set of four, nobody's notes, and made their own threesomes to complete the seven. Among such inventive compilers were Alexander Auld of Ohio, M. L. Swan of Tennessee, Joseph Funk of Virginia, Andrew Johnson of Tennessee, and

William Walker of South Carolina. But the Philadelphian had preëmpted the best primary shapes. His imitators had to make shift with shapes which were far less practicable as note heads. They went on, however, each his own way for some twenty years. In the early seventies Aikin began to see that he would be better off if he made his shapes more available to other song-book producers. And the other compilers not only saw the inherent disadvantages of their own makeshift note shapes but they envisaged the advantages, to all of them, of a united front with a single notation in the entire shape-note field in the face of their now active round-note adversaries. The desired condition was realized beginning with the year 1873. And in a surprisingly short time all seven-shape notations other than the Aikin sort had disappeared.

Aikin's book has been dead long since. But the series of note shapes which he invented is marching on in the little manila-bound books that emerge from more than a score of rural southern print-shops in a total of well over half a million copies a year. These books are used in hundreds of country singing-schools and scores of big singing-conventions. And the singers using these books in the southern states alone must run up into the millions. There probably is a considerable use of the notation elsewhere, too. For some of the publishers tell me that they ship books to every state in the Union. One declared he had made shipments to Europe. The seven-shapers feel quite superior to the "old-timey" four-shapers with whom they have little truck.

I shall add a few observations as to the sorts of songs to which this peculiar notation has clung and as to the influence which it has exerted. All the songs in all the varieties of shape-notation have been and are still religious choral pieces. The old-line "fasola" songs are of two principal sorts: the "fuguing" songs of the domestic New England school exemplified by the compositions of William Billings in the latter part of the eighteenth century,[2] and the "camp-meeting" or "spiritual" songs which appeared in the first decades of the nineteenth century. The fuguing songs, dead everywhere else, are still immensely popular in southern Fasola circles. And the large number of such songs appearing in all editions of the Sacred Harp has been augmented in recent decades by compositions in the same manner by southern rustic musicians. The "spiritual" songs are a body of what was called a hundred years ago the "unwritten music" which grew from the soil, literally, in camp-meeting environments. It was completely unrecorded, that is, as far as the *music* is concerned, before the fasola folk began notating it. They caught the tunes, cobbled three harmonic parts around them, and placed their own names in the right top corner of the page where we usually look for the composer. Thus these singing-school folk became collectors and recorders of a valuable phase of religious folk-song.

The "spiritual" songs are alive today not only among the Sacred Harpers; they are also the main body of song in the books of the Primitive Baptists where they appear in the seven-shape notation. And the ghost of these "white spirituals" walks in the "Negro spirituals," old style.

The seven-shapers by and large have deserted both these older types of song. Their books blossomed out, shortly after the Civil War, in the then new "gospel hymn" type of music. And they have stuck to it, with some little development, ever since. The southern rural song-book compilers now use every year no less than 1500 new songs of this sort, composed by tunesters of their own territory.

---

[2] *Cf. The Musical Quarterly*, April, 1930, "The Rise and Fall of the 'Fugue-Tune' in America," by Edwin Hall Pierce.

The shape-notations may be looked upon as having fulfilled the mission which their originators had in mind. As "singing notes" they have appealed to generations of singers of more or less simple sacred part-songs, and to these alone. They have made singing and learning to read music much easier. And that means that shape-notation has increased popular singing. How much, we can only surmise. The notation has done more. In being allied solely with rurals, and rural institutions, both musical and religious, it has helped to organize and solidify those folk-institutions, folk-mindedness itself, and thus to make the country folk more group-conscious and self-respecting.

But in helping to organize the rural culture, this musical movement has drawn the fire of the natural enemies (natural in America, at least) of ruralism. I refer to the city-controlled church organizations and to the urban musical institutions. Fifty years ago a prominent maker of Methodist hymnals in Nashville called shape-notation "a dangerous delusion." His church soon learned, however, to fight the shape-note devil with holy fire, that fire being a shape-note edition of the authorized hymnal. Today the Publishing House of the Methodist Episcopal Church South prints more shape-note song-books for its country congregations than round-note books for those in the cities.

The urban fosterers of music *comme il faut* became from the start quite put out with their countrified colleagues. It rained epithets. Many an article in the musical magazines of the early post-Civil War period reviled the proponents of "measle-toed" and "square-toed" music, or assured them that their "buckwheat notes" were about "good enough for niggers." The "character-shapes" enthusiasts returned the fire. The editor of the *Musical Million* (chief organ of the country musical-folk, published monthly for over forty years at Dayton in the Valley of Virginia), brought telling sarcasm to bear on the propagandists for the "monkish music" and accused those "round-heads" of trying to put over what was, to his way of thinking, a "foreign language" to the beginner in singing.

Today peace reigns. The country folk—in church, singing-school, and all-day-singing-and-dinner-on-the-grounds—sing from the little 35-cent shape-note books whatever, wherever, and whenever they want to. The urban musician has forgotten his grudge, and even the object of that grudge has passed from his consciousness. The only ones who have a real kick coming are the setters of shape-note music type whose job is about seven times harder than that of the round-note music compositor.

www.ingramcontent.com/pod-product-compliance
Lightning Source LLC
Chambersburg PA
CBHW060544080526
44586CB00012B/851